NRAEF
ManageFirst
PROGRAM®

NRAEF ManageFirst
Controlling Foodservice Costs
Competency Guide

PEARSON
Prentice
Hall

Upper Saddle River, New Jersey 07458

National Restaurant Association
EDUCATIONAL FOUNDATION

Disclaimer

Requests for permission to use or reproduce material from this book should be directed to:

Copyright Permissions
National Restaurant Association Educational Foundation
175 West Jackson Boulevard, Suite 1500
Chicago, IL 60604-2814
312.715.1010
Fax 312.566.9729
Email: permissions@nraef.org

Visit www.nraef.org for information on other National Restaurant Association Educational Foundation products and programs.

NRAEF ManageFirst Program®, NRAEF ManageFirst Professional™, ServSafe®, and ServSafe Alcohol® are either trademarks or registered trademarks of the National Restaurant Association Educational Foundation.

ISBN 10: 0-13-228336-0 (Competency Guide with Examination Answer Sheet)
ISBN 13: 978-0-13-228336-6 (Competency Guide with Examination Answer Sheet)

Printed in the U.S.A.

10 9 8 7 6 5 4 3

Table of Contents

Chapter 5: *Controlling Food Costs in Purchasing and Receiving*

Chapter 6: *Controlling Food Costs in Storage and Issuing*

Chapter 7: *Controlling Food Cost in Production*

Chapter 8: *Controlling Food Cost in Service and Sales*

Chapter 9: *Controlling Labor Costs*

A Message from the National Restaurant Association Educational Foundation

The National Restaurant Association Educational Foundation (NRAEF) is a not-for-profit organization dedicated to fulfilling the educational mission of the National Restaurant Association. We focus on helping the restaurant and foodservice industry address its risk management, recruitment, and retention challenges.

As the nation's largest private-sector employer, the restaurant, hospitality, and foodservice industry is the cornerstone of the American economy, of career-and-employment opportunities, and of local communities. The total economic impact of the restaurant industry is astounding—representing approximately 4 percent of the U.S. gross domestic product. At the NRAEF, we are focused on enhancing this position by providing the valuable tools and resources needed to educate our current and future professionals.

For more information on the NRAEF, please visit our Web site at *www.nraef.org.*

What is the NRAEF ManageFirst Program™?

The NRAEF ManageFirst Program is a management-training certificate program that exemplifies our commitment to developing materials by the industry, for the industry. The program's most powerful strength is that it is based on a set of competencies defined by the restaurant, foodservice, and hospitality industry as critical for success.

NRAEF ManageFirst Program Components

The NRAEF ManageFirst Program includes a set of competency guides, exams, instructor resources, certificates, a new credential, and support activities and services. By participating in the program, you are demonstrating your commitment to becoming a highly qualified professional preparing either to begin or to advance your career in the restaurant, hospitality, and foodservice industry.

The competency guides cover the range of topics listed in the chart at right.

Competency Guide/Exam Topics

NRAEF ManageFirst Core Credential Topics

Hospitality and Restaurant Management

Controlling Foodservice Costs

Human Resources Management and Supervision

ServSafe® Food Safety

NRAEF ManageFirst Foundation Topics

Managerial Accounting

Inventory and Purchasing

Customer Service

Food Production

Menu Marketing and Management

Restaurant Marketing

Nutrition

ServSafe Alcohol™ Responsible Alcohol Service

Within the guides, you will find the essential content for the topic as defined by industry, as well as learning activities, assessments, case studies, suggested field projects, professional profiles, and testimonials. The exam can be administered either online or in a paper and pencil format (see inside front cover for a listing of ISBNs), and it will be proctored. Upon successfully passing the exam, you will be furnished by the NRAEF with a customized certificate. The certificate is a lasting recognition of your accomplishment and a signal to the industry that you have mastered the competency covered within the particular topic.

To earn the NRAEF's new credential, you will be required to pass four core exams and one foundation exam (to be chosen from the remaining program topics) and to document your work experience in the restaurant and foodservice industry. Earning the NRAEF credential is a significant accomplishment.

We applaud you as you either begin or advance your career in the restaurant, hospitality, and foodservice industry. Visit *www.nraef.org* to learn about additional career-building resources offered by the NRAEF, including scholarships for college students enrolled in relevant industry programs.

NRAEF ManageFirst Program Ordering Information

Review copies or support materials:
FACULTY FIELD SERVICES
Tel: 800.526.0485

Domestic orders and inquiries:
PEARSON CUSTOMER SERVICE
Tel: 800.922.0579
www.prenhall.com

International orders and inquiries:
U.S. EXPORT SALES OFFICE
Pearson Education International Customer Service Group
200 Old Tappan Road
Old Tappan, NJ 07675 USA
Tel: 201.767.5021
Fax: 201.767.5625

For corporate, government and special sales (consultants, corporations, training centers, VARs, and corporate resellers) orders and inquiries:
PEARSON CORPORATE SALES
Tel: 317.428.3411
Fax: 317.428.3343
Email: managefirst@prenhall.com

For additional information regarding other Prentice Hall publications, instructor and student support materials, locating your sales representative and much more, please visit *www.prenhall.com/managefirst.*

Acknowledgements

The National Restaurant Association Educational Foundation is grateful for the significant contributions made to this competency guide by the following individuals.

John A. Drysdale, MS, FMP

In addition, we are pleased to thank our many other advisors, subject matter experts, reviewers, and contributors for their time, effort, and dedication to this program.

Teresa Marie Gargano
  Adamski

Ernest Boger

Robert Bosselman

Jerald Chesser

Cynthia Deale

Fred DeMicco

Johnathan Deustch

Gene Fritz

John Gescheidle

Thomas Hamilton

John Hart

Thomas Kaltenecker

Ray Kavanaugh

John Kidwell

Carol Kizer

Holly Ruttan Maloney

Cynthia Mayo

Fred Mayo

Patrick Moreo

Robert O'Halloran

Brian O'Malley

Terrence Pappas

James Perry

Patricia Plavcan

William N. Reynolds

Rosenthal Group

Mokie Steiskal

Karl Titz

Terry Umbreit

David Wightman

Deanne Williams

Mike Zema

Renee Zonka

Features of the NRAEF ManageFirst Competency Guides

We have designed the NRAEF ManageFirst Competency Guides to enhance your ability to learn and retain important information that is critical to this restaurant and foodservice industry function. Here are the key features you will find within this guide.

Beginning Each Guide

Tuning In to You

When you open an NRAEF ManageFirst Competency Guide for the first time, you might ask yourself: Why do I need to know about this topic? Every topic of these guides involves key information you will need as you manage a restaurant or foodservice operation. Located in the front of each review guide, "Tuning In to You" is a brief synopsis that illustrates some of the reasons the information contained throughout that particular guide is important to you. It exemplifies real-life scenarios that you will face as a manager and how the concepts in the book will help you in your career.

Professional Profile

This is your opportunity to meet a professional who is currently working in the field associated with a competency guide's topic. This person's story will help you gain insight into the responsibilities related to his or her position, as well as the training and educational history linked to it. You will also see the daily and cumulative impact this position has on an operation, and receive advice from a person who has successfully met the challenges of being a manager.

Beginning Each Chapter

Inside This Chapter

Chapter content is organized under these major headings.

Learning Objectives

Learning objectives identify what you should be able to do after completing each chapter. These objectives are linked to the required tasks a manager must be able to perform in relation to the function discussed in the competency guide.

Test Your Knowledge

Each chapter begins with some True or False questions designed to test your prior knowledge of some of the concepts presented in the chapter. The answers to these questions, as well as the concepts behind them, can be found within the chapter—see the page reference after each question.

Key Terms

These terms are important for thorough understanding of the chapter's content. They are highlighted throughout the chapter, where they are explicitly defined or their meaning is made clear within the paragraphs in which they appear.

Throughout Each Chapter

Exhibits

Exhibits are placed throughout each chapter to visually reinforce the key concepts presented in the text. Types of exhibits include charts, tables, photographs, and illustrations.

Think About It…

These thought-provoking sidebars reveal supportive information about the section they appear beside.

Activities

Apply what you have learned throughout the chapter by completing the various activities in the text. The activities have been designed to give you additional practice and better understanding of the concepts addressed in the learning objectives. Types of activities include case studies, role-plays, and problem solving, among others.

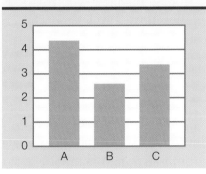

Exhibit

Exhibits are visuals that will help you learn about key concepts.

Think About It...

Consider these supplemental insights as you read through a chapter.

Activity

Activity

Types of activities you will complete include case studies, role-plays, and problem solving, among others.

At the End of Each Chapter

Review Your Learning

These multiple-choice or open- or close-ended questions or problems are designed to test your knowledge of the concepts presented in the chapter. These questions have been aligned with the objectives and should provide you with an opportunity to practice or apply the content that supports these objectives. If you have difficulty answering them, you should review the content further.

At the End of the Guide

Field Project

This real-world project gives you the valuable opportunity to apply many of the concepts you will learn in a competency guide. You will interact with industry practitioners, enhance your knowledge, and research, apply, analyze, evaluate, and report on your findings. It will provide you with an in-depth "reality check" of the policies and practices of this management function.

Tuning In to You

To stay in business, a restaurant or foodservice establishment must make a profit. Even when there are changes in outside circumstances, such as the economy or the competition, an effective manager should be able to control foodservice costs so that an operation will stay afloat. Think about this example:

Sarah has just been promoted to a back-of-the-house manager at a local restaurant in a small town. One of her new responsibilities is to track and maintain the cost of spoilage from the kitchen. The previous manager had no standard for tracking the spoilage costs, and so as part of her new job, Sarah establishes a standard procedure for tracking food spoilage per day. She is then able to better understand the waste per week and sets up preventative measures within the purchasing function to avoid excess spoilage. Because of Sarah's standard procedure for tracking food spoilage, the weekly cost of food is reduced, and revenue is added to the weekly budget.

While this may seem like a general example, it is not an arbitrary one. At its essence, controlling foodservice costs is about management paying attention to all aspects of the operation, including inventory, food costs, budget, storage, staff scheduling, benefits, payroll, waste, menu, purchasing, and receiving. Since there is so much information that needs to be tracked, detailed paperwork and records must be kept so that good decisions can be made. Management must also know how to analyze market data and understand how current budgets correspond with historical numbers.

Done correctly and on a continued basis, cost control by management will ensure that an operation stays profitable on a day-to-day basis. For example, if cost control standards are upheld properly and consistently, staff turnover will be low, and this will decrease the high cost of hiring and training new staff. In addition, food costs, spoilage, and waste will be minimal because of standards and inventory controls that are in place. Cost control standards also ensure that customers have a positive experience that exceeds their expectations. Taking this idea one step further, it is natural to assume that these satisfied customers will become loyal ones and will increase business (and profit) by word of mouth. Cost control should not only help a restaurant stay afloat on a day-to-day basis, but should also help keep the entire environment up to par—ideally, the food will be fresh, staff will be well compensated and friendly, cleanliness and spoilage will be controlled, and the menu will offer attractive options that are appropriately priced. So, although controlling costs may seem to be only about budget and finances, it comes full circle to affect the core of the operation's product and image and ultimately determines the customer's opinions and level of satisfaction with the restaurant or foodservice operation.

Professional Profile
Your opportunity to meet someone working in the field

John Geiger

Vice President
Anderson Restaurant Group
Kansas City, MO

My name is John Geiger and I am currently the vice president of the Anderson Restaurant Group. I graduated from high school in a suburb of Kansas City in 1981. While I attended high school, I washed dishes, bussed tables, and sold hot dogs. In 1983, I graduated from Johnson County Community College with an Associate of Arts degree in Hotel and Restaurant Management. While I was attending college, I worked for a national hotel chain as a front desk clerk, night auditor, and banquet captain. After graduation, I went on to get my Bachelor of Science degree at the Conrad Hilton College of Hotel and Restaurant Management at the University of Houston. I financed my college education by bartending at a prestigious yacht club in Clear Lake, Texas. Upon graduation, I advanced to bar manager and was responsible for a club that generated over 1.5 million dollars in liquor, beer, and wine sales. After marriage, I returned in 1986 to Kansas City to pursue my career with an independent restaurant operator.

The Anderson Restaurant Group has grown from one restaurant in 1987, the Hereford House, to eight operations in 2005. The original Hereford House opened in 1957 and was acquired by Rod Anderson in 1987. It is positioned as a midrange steakhouse offering complete entrées with steak, salad, and side dish. The average check runs about $28 per person for dinner. Our beef is Midwest raised, corn fed, and processed through one vendor in Skyler, Nebraska. The steaks are all hand cut in-house, are aged twenty-eight days or more, and are charcoal grilled, giving them a unique flavor.

I began working as the general manager for the Hereford House in 1996 when the second operation was opened in Leawood, Kansas. Since then, we have added three more Hereford House restaurants: Pierpont's at Union Station (upscale, fresh seafood, and prime steaks), Java Time at Union Station (coffee house), and the Hollywood Room by Hereford House (off-site and banquet facility). In addition to these operations, we also hold a management contract on Harry's Country Club, a honky-tonk bar in the River Market district of Kansas City.

The restaurant business is a business of details, including pennies, nickels, and dimes. Attention to detail is what sets one restaurant apart from another. Accounting is one of those details that needs to be looked at every day, through sales and its relationship to cost. The paradox with controlling cost is that costs mean nothing if you do not have sales.

For any business, it is very important to understand accounting concepts because the objective is to take in more money (revenue) than the money you spend (expenses). The restaurant business is unique because it is the one of the few industries that works with a raw product that comes in the back door, goes into storage, transitions into production, and is sold and delivered to the customer all under one roof. Any restaurateur should be cognitive of costs and cost controls because they are vital to the restaurant business. I strongly urge anyone going into the restaurant business to have a very good understanding of them.

Introduction

My advice to any potential restaurant entrepreneur is to explore college curriculum regarding restaurant management, read and understand textbooks designed for cost and cost controls, gain industry experience, read trade magazines, and be able to apply theories in actual real-world settings. Accounting in school sometimes seems ambiguous and irrelevant; however, it is important to have this basic knowledge to be successful in business. Although mundane to some, the knowledge and understanding of debits, credits, costs, cost controls, sales, profit and loss statements, balance sheets, and inventories are essential to a successful restaurateur.

As part of my financial responsibilities, I review our prime costs, which are for product and labor. Food and bar costs are controlled through standardized recipes, portion control, purchasing standards, menu and sales mix, perpetual inventories, inventory turns, and daily sensitive inventories. Labor is a cost that needs to be monitored every shift, and if possible, every hour. It should be analyzed by dollars and hours in relationship to sales. This is a scoreboard that should measure the efficiency of any operation and can be easily compared operation to operation. These are just a few examples of cost controls that I look at on a daily basis.

Another significant detail that needs regular reviewing is the potential for internal theft or waste. Although we would like to think all of our employees are trustworthy, it is not always the case, so I try to create systems that take away the temptation for thievery.

My present goal is to ensure profitability and increased sales for the restaurant operations. My current job is delegating, coordinating, planning, and scheduling all of the management staff functions in our restaurants. The understanding of accounting, cost controls, and details is what makes the achievement of my goals possible. I cannot stress enough how important it is to have a substantial knowledge of these subjects. I am continually educating myself through trade magazines, online courses, and the restaurant association. I am past president of the Greater Kansas City Restaurant Association and feel that the relationships that I have established through this association have furthered my knowledge. Someday I would like to share my experiences of the restaurant industry with students on the college level.

To learn more about the Anderson Restaurant Group or me, please visit us at *www.herefordhouse.com.*

What Is Cost Control?

Inside This Chapter

- ■ The Manager's Role in Cost Control
- ■ Types of Costs
- ■ The Cost Control Process

After completing this chapter, you should be able to:

- ■ Describe the relationship between standards and controlling costs.
- ■ Identify the types of costs incurred by a restaurant or foodservice organization.
- ■ Classify foodservice costs as controllable or noncontrollable.
- ■ Describe and give examples of controllable and noncontrollable costs.
- ■ Classify foodservice costs as variable, semivariable, or fixed.
- ■ Describe and give examples of variable, semivariable, and fixed costs.
- ■ Explain the basic foodservice cost control process.

Test Your Knowledge

1. **True or False:** Standards apply to the entire spectrum of the restaurant business. *(See p. 3.)*

2. **True or False:** Prime cost refers to the cost of prime steaks while choice cost refers to the cost of choice steaks. *(See p. 9.)*

3. **True or False:** To maintain profitability, cost controls must be installed at all stages of the operation. *(See p. 3.)*

4. **True or False:** Understanding the different types of costs is key to making effective cost control decisions. *(See p. 4.)*

5. **True or False:** The income statement is an important managerial tool for analyzing costs. *(See p. 10.)*

6. **True or False:** Another name for the income statement is the profit and loss report. *(See p. 10.)*

Key Terms

Control	Income statement	Profit
Controllable cost	Labor expense	Sales
Corrective action	Line item review	Semivariable cost
Cost of food sold	Loss	Standard
Fixed cost	Noncontrollable cost	Total expense
Gross profit	Prime cost	Variable cost

Introduction

Restaurant management involves thousands of details, and each of these details can affect the overall performance of the operation. This is especially true in the area of controlling costs. It is truly one of the most important functions of restaurant management.

The Manager's Role in Cost Control

In most restaurant or foodservice operations, managers take personal charge of an operation's cost control process; however, the size and scope of an operation will determine the extent to which its managers exercise direct control or delegate that responsibility to other staff. Regardless of the type of operation you manage, in order to be effective, you must fully understand all the costs associated with running the business. Cost control is not something that can be done once and only followed up with occasionally. If costs get out of line, the profitability of a restaurant could be seriously jeopardized. Managers must monitor and control costs on a daily basis, sometimes even on an hourly or minute-by-minute basis.

The Importance of Controls

In every area of a restaurant or foodservice operation, controls are an important part of making a profit. A **control** is a method of exercising some amount of power over events or situations in order to achieve a particular result. At every stage of operations, controls need to be established to prevent problems and achieve the goals of the organization. Cost controls start with the menu and continue on through purchasing, receiving, storage, production, and finally, service. Without controls in place, an operation has no way of determining and evaluating whether the operation is profitable or meeting its budget. Controlling and reducing costs are desirable trends for ensuring the ongoing financial health of an operation.

People often use various controls to regulate their actions in daily life. For example, many people regulate the amount of fatty food they eat to achieve a desired healthy state of being, and when people are in the process of watching what they eat, limitations or restrictions become part of the method to achieve that desired state. Similarly, companies often create policies and procedures that govern how employees behave. In these examples, there are consequences associated with choosing not to follow the established regulations. If someone eats too much fatty food, he or she might develop various health-related illnesses; if a person does not follow policies at work, there is the chance that he or she will be reprimanded or terminated.

Think About It...

It has been said that success is the sum of the details. Why would a successful manager need to understand the importance of controlling details?

Cost Control Standards

So how do you know if the cost controls in place are achieving the desired results? The actual results must be checked against a standard. A **standard** is a measure that is established to compare levels of attainment for a goal or a measure of adequacy. Standards are levels of excellence against which results are evaluated. People use standards in their daily lives, usually without even thinking about it. They buy one brand of gas over another because that brand meets their standard. They vacuum the carpet because they have a standard for cleanliness.

Restaurant operations also have standards. In the restaurant and foodservice industry, managers, employees, and suppliers are expected to meet the standards set by management. Standards cover the entire spectrum of the business—sales, quality, quantity, production, service, employment, and so on. Standards are an integral part of the process of controlling costs. When management sets standards for costs, they do so with the understanding that those standards will produce a profit for the business. Cost control standards direct managers in every aspect of restaurant management and operations, from initial menu planning all the way through to purchasing, receiving, storing, production, service, scheduling staff, and cash handling.

Cost standards vary from one type of operation to another. Even within chain operations, the cost standards might vary from region to region. Consider that in some operations—such as restaurants, catering companies, and hotels—the intent is to make a profit, while in other foodservice operations—such as hospitals, nursing homes, schools, and prisons—the objective is to meet budget.

Whether the intent of the business is to make money or to stay within budget, costs must be controlled. The standard is the regulating force behind controlling costs. It is the responsibility of management to understand the standards for the operation and then determine ways to control various factors to maintain or exceed the standards. Ideally, if standards are consistently met, the restaurant will be profitable.

Types of Costs

Many different types of costs are involved when running a restaurant or foodservice operation. They can be classified in different ways. The most common classifications are controllable and noncontrollable costs, and fixed, variable, and semivariable costs. The reason for classifying costs is to differentiate between the ones that management can and cannot control. Identifying and understanding different types of costs helps managers interpret cost-related information and make control-related decisions. See *Exhibit 1a* for examples of controllable and noncontrollable costs.

Exhibit 1a

Controllable and Noncontrollable Costs

Gross profit	Total:	$ 13,765	$ 20,655	$ 27,535	$ 34,420	$ 41,300
Controllable expenses						
Salaries and wages		7,050	9,910	13,215	16,520	18,500
Direct		1,320	1,980	2,645	3,305	3,965
Utilities		1,250	1,250	1,250	1,250	1,250
Marketing		500	500	500	500	500
Administrative		1,000	1,000	1,000	1,000	1,000
Repairs and maintenance		1,000	1,000	1,000	1,000	1,000
	Total:	$ 12,120	$ 15,640	$ 19,610	$ 23,575	$ 26,215
Noncontrollable expenses						
Occupation expenses		$ 2,500	$ 2,500	$ 2,500	$ 2,500	$ 2,500
Interest expenses		160	215	270	270	270
	Total:	$ 2,660	$ 2,715	$ 2,770	$ 2,770	$ 2,770
Total expenses	Total:	$ 14,780	$ 18,355	$ 22,380	$ 26,345	$ 28,985

Notice how controllable and noncontrollable costs are expressed on the operating budget.

Controllable and Noncontrollable Costs

One method of classifying costs is to categorize them as either controllable costs or noncontrollable costs. **Controllable costs** are those costs that management can directly control. **Noncontrollable costs** are those costs over which management has little or no control.

Controllable Costs

An example of a controllable cost is food cost. Management can control this cost by using standardized recipes or exercising standard procedures for portion control, menu listing, and pricing, or by one of several other restraints. For example, if the price of chicken increases and no action is taken, the restaurant's food cost will increase. At this point, management can either raise the selling price of all chicken entrées, reduce portions, reposition the items on the menu, or eliminate chicken from the menu altogether. By taking action, management has controlled the increased cost of chicken, resulting in no increase in the restaurant's food cost.

Another example of a controllable cost is labor cost. By changing the number of hours an employee works, a manager can affect labor costs. For example, if a restaurant's sales drop, and no action is taken, payroll cost as a percentage of sales increases. By reducing the number of hours worked by employees, this percentage could be brought back into line.

It should be pointed out, however, that in exercising these options, management must always be careful not to alienate customers. If the selling price of chicken entrées is increased too much, or too many hours are trimmed off the schedule, resulting in poor service, customers could be driven to the competition.

Noncontrollable Costs

An example of a noncontrollable cost is insurance. Once an insurance policy has been negotiated, management has no control over the cost of that policy. Another example is license fees. Management has no control over the rate charged for bar or occupation licenses. A third example is the operation's lease or mortgage. Once signed, management has virtually no control over this cost.

Activity

Cost Cutting Practice

Julia is reviewing a list of expenses for the operation of her restaurant. She notices several jumps in costs compared to the previous month. The items that have increased in cost are:

- Electricity
- Gas
- Produce delivery fees
- Milk

Given this information, answer the following:

1 What can Julia do to reduce these costs in the upcoming months?

_____

_____

2 How might these changes affect the restaurant's customers?

_____

_____

3 Are there any costs that Julia cannot reduce?

_____

_____

_____

Fixed, Variable, and Semivariable Costs

Fixed, variable, or semivariable costs are based on each cost's relationship to sales volume. In other words, does a cost increase or decrease as sales increase or decrease or does the cost remain the same regardless of sales volume?

Fixed costs

Fixed costs are those costs that remain the same regardless of sales volume. Insurance is an example of a fixed cost. As previously stated, once the insurance policies have been negotiated, the cost remains the same throughout the term of the policy. For example, if the cost of insuring the business is $1,000 per month, it will remain at $1,000 every month. If the restaurant has sales of $10,000 one month, $20,000 the next month, and $15,000 the following month, the insurance cost remains the same at $1,000 per month. It does not change when restaurant sales change.

Variable costs

Variable costs increase and decrease in direct proportion to sales. Food cost is one example. As sales increase, more food is purchased to replenish inventory, and as sales decrease, less food is purchased. If adequate controls are in place and there is little waste or theft, the amount of food used is in direct proportion to sales.

Semivariable costs

Semivariable costs increase and decrease as sales increase and decrease but not in direct proportion. They are made up of both fixed costs and variable costs. Labor cost is an example. (See *Exhibit 1b*.) Management is normally paid a salary that remains the same regardless of the operation's sales volume. If the general manager and the chef are collectively paid $120,000 per year, they will receive that amount regardless of whether the restaurant brings in $1,000,000 or $1,300,000 per year. Thus, management's salary is a fixed cost.

On the other hand, staff such as the waitstaff and line cooks are paid hourly wages and are scheduled according to anticipated sales. As a result, the cost of hourly staff increases as sales increase and decreases as sales decrease. If proper scheduling is used, the cost will increase and decrease in direct proportion to sales.

Putting this all together, labor is a semivariable cost because there is a fixed cost component (management's salary) and a variable cost component (hourly staff wages). The left-hand graph in *Exhibit 1c* shows how variable costs change in *direct* relationship to sales volume. The right-hand graph shows that although semivariable costs also change with sales volume, they do not change in direct relationship with sales.

Exhibit 1b

Labor is considered a semivariable cost because it has a fixed component (salaried employees), as well as a variable component (hourly employees).

Exhibit 1c

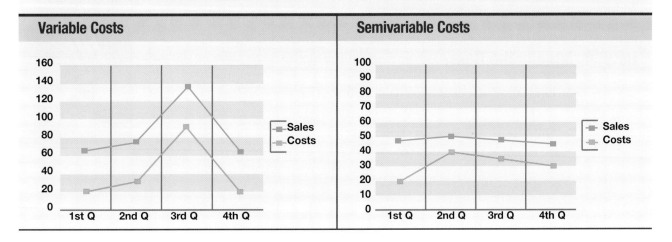

Variable Costs and Semivariable Costs in Relation to Sales Volume

Crossover of Cost Classifications

Clearly, there is some crossover in classifying costs. Variable and semivariable costs are usually controllable costs. Fixed costs are typically noncontrollable costs. While there are some exceptions to this, for the most part it is true.

Another thing to consider is that a particular cost could be classified differently depending on how it is budgeted. For example, if a restaurant's lease is negotiated at $3,000 per month, rent is a fixed cost. It does not increase or decrease according to sales volume. It will always be $3,000. If, on the other hand, the lease is negotiated at 6 percent of sales, rent is then a variable cost. The amount will increase or decrease in direct proportion to sales volume.

Another possibility is that the lease calls for a monthly payment of $1,000 plus 3 percent of sales. In this case, rent is a semivariable cost. The $1,000 is paid regardless of sales volume, making it a fixed cost. The variable part of the cost comes from the 3 percent of sales, which increases or decreases as sales increase or decrease in direct proportion. As discussed earlier, a cost with both fixed and variable attributes is a semivariable cost. It increases and decreases as sales increase and decrease, but not in direct proportion.

From this example, it can be seen that some costs, depending on how they are structured, can be classified as either fixed, variable, or semivariable. This is also a good example of the exception to the rule stated previously—variable and semivariable costs are normally controllable. In this case, these costs are noncontrollable because the lease cannot be changed until it expires; thus management has no control over the lease payment.

Another example is advertising. If management determines that they will spend 2 percent of sales on advertising, it is then a variable cost. It will increase and decrease in direct proportion to sales. If, on the other hand, they decide to spend $2,500 per month on advertising, it is then a fixed cost. It will not change as sales volume changes.

Activity

How Variable Is the Cost?

Classify each cost listed as either *fixed* (f), *variable* (v), or *semivariable* (s).

_____ **1** Electricity   _____ **4** Insurance

_____ **2** Wages   _____ **5** Rent

_____ **3** Beverages   _____ **6** Food

Prime Cost

The two largest costs that management has to control are food cost and labor cost. Together they are known as the **prime cost**—the two highest costs in the operation. The rule of thumb regarding prime cost is that it should not exceed 65 percent of sales. Thus, if a restaurant has a high food cost, it must have a low labor cost. For example, a steakhouse could run a 43 percent food cost and a 20 percent labor cost, while a quick-service operation could run a 25 percent food cost and a 35 percent labor cost. Either way, the prime cost is below 65 percent.

Although controlling prime cost is a major responsibility for managers, a word of caution is needed. Sometimes management, in their zeal to control things, carries controlling costs too far. Controls are important, but not to the point of interfering with one of the primary objectives of the restaurant, which is to build sales. Sometimes controls slow down production or service. When this happens, it is time to review the control and change it so that service (and ultimately sales) will not suffer. Another point to remember is cost. A control should not cost more than what it is intended to control. If a few customers in a quick-service operation were taking a handful of mustard packets, it would not be cost effective to hire a security guard to watch over the condiment stand. While this illustration is extreme, management sometimes overreacts and ends up overcontrolling a situation to their own detriment.

The Cost Control Process

Taking action to reduce operating costs requires understanding which costs might be unnecessary and deciding what can be done to eliminate them. At the same time, any controls implemented must ensure continuation of the operation's standard levels for safety, sanitation, and customer service. With experience, managers learn to quickly spot cost-related concerns in their operations.

Step 1: Collect Accurate Sales and Cost Data

Historical sales information is just as important to cost control as it is to other management functions. The relationship between sales and the costs that were incurred to achieve those actual sales is often proportional, and many foodservice costs change depending on sales volume. In order to know whether costs are within an appropriate range, it is imperative to start with accurate sales information.

Sales should be tracked for different periods, including yearly, monthly, weekly, daily, meal period, and even hourly.

■ Yearly and monthly data are used for budgeting and income statement purposes.

■ Weekly and daily sales data are used for purchasing and scheduling.

■ Daily and meal period data are also used for scheduling and production planning.

Sales information can come from several sources. Yearly and monthly sales information comes from the income statement. Hourly, daily, and weekly figures are usually generated by point-of-sale (POS) system reports. In operations without POS systems, it is tabulated from guest checks or periodic cash register readings.

In addition to having accurate sales information, it is also necessary to have accurate cost information. Most cost information can be taken from operational records. Many POS systems track inventory, food waste, and employee work hours. Management can usually run reports of inventory and food costs, payroll costs, and actual labor hours.

Exhibit 1d

Sample Abbreviated Income Statement

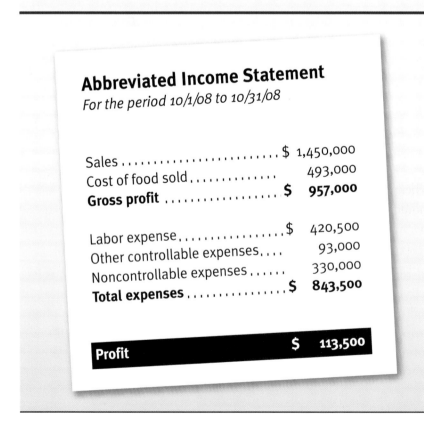

Abbreviated Income Statement
For the period 10/1/08 to 10/31/08

Sales	$ 1,450,000
Cost of food sold	493,000
Gross profit	**$ 957,000**
Labor expense	$ 420,500
Other controllable expenses	93,000
Noncontrollable expenses	330,000
Total expenses	**$ 843,500**
Profit	**$ 113,500**

The Income Statement as a Cost Control Tool

The best way to tell at a glance how an operation is performing is by reading its income statement. An **income statement** is a report showing sales, costs, and the profit or loss of a business. It also shows whether an operation made or lost money during the report's time period. The income statement, also called the profit and loss report, is a valuable tool. It helps managers gauge an operation's profitability and compare results to goals or standards. Monitoring these reports helps management determine areas where controls are needed to bring the business up to its standards.

In the abbreviated income statement shown in *Exhibit 1d,*

you will see that each line represents typical information included on an income statement.

- **Sales** is the dollar amount the restaurant has taken in for food.

- **Cost of food sold** shows the dollar amount spent on that food. It is the opening inventory plus purchases, minus the ending inventory.

- **Gross profit** is the amount of money made on the cost of food sold. It is figured by subtracting the cost of food sold from sales.

- **Labor expense** is the payroll for hourly employees and salaried management. It also includes FICA and Medicare payments and employee benefit costs (sick days, holidays, health insurance, etc.).

- Other controllable expenses include such items as paper and cleaning supplies.

- Noncontrollable expenses cover such items as rent and utilities.

- **Total expenses** include labor, controllable, and noncontrollable expenses.

- **Profit** is what remains after all expenses are paid. It is figured by subtracting total expenses from gross profit or by subtracting total expenses and food cost from sales. Sales must exceed costs for an operation to stay profitable. Conversely, an operation experiences a loss when its expenses are greater than its sales.

Step 2: Monitor and Analyze Sales and Costs

Once actual sales and costs are calculated, these figures are monitored and compared to budgeted amounts, operational standards, and historical information to identify any variances. This should be done on a regular basis. It is a good way to check how your operation is running and to prevent future problems by catching them early.

Every item on the budget should be checked against actual figures, and the difference should be noted. This is called a **line item review.** When the budget is compared to the actual figures, each item's number should match or be very close to the figures. Any difference between the budget and the actual amounts may be expressed as a dollar amount and/or percentage. A format for comparing budgeted and actual amounts using a line item review is illustrated in *Exhibit 1e.*

Exhibit 1e

Sample Line Item Review

Budget Item	$ Budgeted	$ Actual	$ Difference	% Difference
Food sales	$100,000	$90,000	$10,000	−10%

As discussed earlier, all restaurant chains and most independent restaurant operators have standards or goals they want to achieve. In the case of controlling costs, the standard represents the level at which a cost *should be.* Standard costs are carefully calculated to ensure that the operation achieves profitability while maintaining expected customer service levels.

For example, maintaining proper customer service levels requires the operation to have the appropriate level of labor on site at all times. With this consideration, management compares the actual labor cost percentage to the standard labor cost percentage for the operation. The standard labor cost percentage, if determined correctly, takes into account the level of service at which management expects its operation to perform. Sufficient hours scheduled in the kitchen will result in an excellent product being served in a prompt manner. Likewise, the correct number of servers in the dining room to take orders and serve efficiently will carry out the company's mission of good food and good service.

Remember that management determines a standard based on many factors, not the least of which is profit. When considering a labor standard, the goal of management is to produce a quality product and provide quality service. To go below the standard could sacrifice product quality or service excellence. For this reason, it is just as important to come up to the standard as it is to come down to the standard.

In addition to comparing actual costs to standard costs, management also compares actual costs to historical costs, which are costs that have incurred in the past. By comparing these two figures, management can see if the operation is improving or regressing.

When comparing actual costs to historical costs, it is important to remember that similar periods must be compared. Thus, January's labor cost is compared to January's labor cost of the previous year, and Monday's sales this week are compared to Monday's sales of last week. Special events or unusual circumstances should also be taken into account when comparing historical costs. For example, comparing this Sunday's sales to last Sunday's (which happened to be Mother's Day) would not be a good comparison. A heavy noontime rainstorm could increase the sales in an employee cafeteria located in an office building, and decrease the sales in a restaurant across the street from the building.

Think About It...

There are numerous restaurant inventory software programs on the market. How might cost control software be used to dramatically reduce food and beverage costs?

Step 3: Take Corrective Action as Appropriate

Over time, even small changes in costs can add up to significant losses. When costs are out of line, the cause should be investigated.

If the budget and actual values do not match, they must be analyzed to see what might have gone wrong. If there is a variance, action should be taken to correct it. For example, if food cost is off, purchasing, preparation, and receiving procedures should be reviewed. If labor cost is off, scheduling and production standards should be analyzed.

As soon as the cause for a variance is identified, the manager should take steps to correct the problem, or **corrective actions**. For example, if sales are lower than expected, the hours on the employee work schedule might need to be reduced to lower labor costs. *Exhibit 1f* lists some examples of corrective actions that can be taken to control various costs. As discussed earlier, managers have more control over some costs than they do over others. Corrective actions can only be used to affect controllable costs.

In addition to taking corrective actions, it may also be necessary to reforecast and make changes to the operating budget. As circumstances change, some forecasts used to prepare the original budget may no longer be accurate. Reviewing forecasts, at least on a monthly basis, will help managers make realistic adjustments to the budget for upcoming periods.

Exhibit 1f

Sample Corrective Actions for Cost Control

To Reduce	Implement These Corrective Actions
Food cost	■ Reduce portion size. ■ Replace food item with a more cost-effective ingredient. ■ Feature items with higher profit margins. ■ Raise menu prices.
Food waste	■ Monitor portion control. ■ Monitor food storage and rotation. ■ Monitor food ordering. ■ Improve communication to reduce production errors.
Inventory cost	■ Order appropriate quantities—avoid having too much or too little in storage.
Labor cost	■ Reduce number of employees on schedule. ■ Ask employees to end their shifts early. ■ Schedule cross-trained staff (for example, server/cashier/hostess).

Activity

Evaluating Cost Control Software

The Web sites listed below offer various types of software programs for controlling costs. Visit the sites and select at least three different programs that deal with cost control and compare them. Decide what criteria you will use to compare these software programs. You must have at least four different criteria; "price," for example. Set up a table on a separate piece of paper to show the data you selected for comparison.

■ *www.foodtrak.com*

■ *www.restaurantplus.com*

■ *www.foodsoftware.com*

If you had to make a choice based on these criteria, which program would you select and why?

_____

_____

_____

_____

_____

_____

Summary

In most restaurant or foodservice operations, managers take personal charge of an operation's cost control process; however, the size and scope of an operation will determine the extent to which its managers exercise direct control or delegate that responsibility to other staff. If costs get out of line, the profitability of a restaurant could be seriously jeopardized.

At every stage of operations, controls need to be set up to prevent problems and to achieve the goals of the organization. Cost controls start with the menu and continue on through purchasing to receiving, storage, production, and finally, service. Without controls in place, an operation has no way of determining and evaluating whether the operation is profitable or meeting its budget. Controlling and reducing costs are both desirable trends for ensuring the ongoing financial health of an operation.

A standard is a measure that is established to compare levels of attainment for a goal or a measure of adequacy. In the restaurant and foodservice industry, managers, employees, and suppliers are expected to meet the standards set by management. Standards cover the entire spectrum of the restaurant business.

Cost standards vary from one type of operation to another. Costs can be classified in different ways. In the restaurant and foodservice industry, the most common classifications are controllable and noncontrollable costs, as well as fixed, variable, and semivariable costs. The reason for classifying costs is to differentiate between the ones that management can control and those that cannot be controlled. Identifying and understanding these different types of costs help managers interpret cost-related information and make control-related decisions.

Controllable costs are those costs that management can directly control. Noncontrollable costs are those costs over which management has little or no control. Fixed costs are those costs that remain the same regardless of sales volume, while variable costs increase or decrease in direct proportion to increases or decreases in sales volume. Conversely, semivariable costs increase and decrease as sales increase and decrease, but not in direct proportion. Semivariable costs are made up of both fixed costs and variable costs. The two largest costs that management has to control are food cost and labor cost. Together they are known as the prime cost, because these are the two highest costs in the operation.

With experience, managers learn to quickly spot cost-related concerns in their operations. The best way to tell at a glance how an operation is performing is by reading its income statement. Once actual sales and costs are calculated, these figures are monitored and compared to budgeted amounts, operational standards, and historical information in order to identify any variances. When costs are determined to be out of line, the cause should be investigated, and if there is a variance, management should take action to correct the problem causing the variance.

Review Your Learning

1 Which of the following is true about standards?

  A. Standards are used as a basis for comparison.

  B. The use of standards to measure costs is optional.

  C. Standards are the same across the industry.

  D. If standards are consistently met, an operation will not grow its business.

2 Which is a controllable cost?

  A. Labor   C. Insurance

  B. License   D. Property tax

3 Which is a noncontrollable cost?

  A. Rent   C. Advertising

  B. Food   D. Hourly wages

4 Labor cost is an example of a

  A. variable cost.

  B. semivariable cost.

  C. fixed cost.

  D. noncontrollable cost.

5 A cost that increases or decreases as sales increase or decrease and does so in direct proportion is known as a

  A. variable cost.

  B. semivariable cost.

  C. fixed cost.

  D. noncontrollable cost.

6 When discussing labor cost,

  A. management is usually a fixed cost.

  B. hourly staff are a variable cost.

  C. Both A and B

  D. Neither A nor B

7 A cost that increases or decreases as sales increase or decrease, but *not* in direct proportion is known as a

  A. semivariable cost.

  B. variable cost.

  C. fixed cost.

  D. noncontrollable cost.

8 Of the following costs, which is the most important for the restaurant or foodservice manager to control?

  A. Rent

  B. Equipment

  C. Fixed costs

  D. Prime cost

9 Which of the following is the first step in the cost control process?

  A. Analyze costs

  B. Take corrective action

  C. Prepare a line-item review

  D. Collect sales and cost data

10 Analyzing costs includes which of the following comparisons?

  A. Comparison between actual costs and standard costs

  B. Comparison between actual costs and historical costs

  C. Comparison between actual costs and budgeted costs

  D. All of the above

A Closer Look at Food Cost

2

Inside This Chapter

- Food Cost Defined
- Calculating Food Cost
- Calculating Food Cost Percentage

After completing this chapter, you should be able to:

- Calculate food cost and food cost percentage.
- Explain the effect that cost and sales have on food cost percentage.

Test Your Knowledge

1 **True or False:** When food is purchased and received, it immediately becomes part of food cost. *(See p. 18.)*

2 **True or False:** Food cost includes food used to provide employee meals. *(See p. 19.)*

3 **True or False:** Opening inventory is the same number as the closing inventory of the previous period. *(See p. 20.)*

4 **True or False:** Food cost percentage is obtained by dividing food cost by sales. *(See p. 22.)*

5 **True or False:** Because food cost is a variable expense, it always increases and decreases as sales increase or decease and does so in direct proportion. *(See p. 23.)*

Key Terms

Closing inventory	Opening inventory
Food cost	Purchases
Food cost percentage	Total food available
Inventory	

Introduction

What exactly is food cost? Many people, including some restaurant managers, have a misconception that when food is purchased it becomes food cost. This is not true. It is true that purchases are an integral part of food cost; however, food cost is actually the amount of food that is used. Only in extremely rare cases is all of the food that has been purchased actually used.

Food Cost Defined

Food cost is the actual dollar value of the food used by an operation during a certain period. It includes the expense incurred when food is consumed for any reason. Food cost includes the cost of food sold, given away, wasted, or even stolen. *(See Exhibit 2a).*

Some restaurant or foodservice operations will further refine cost of food sold to get a more accurate number of how all the food is being used. To do this, the operation would subtract the following items from cost of food sold:

- **Employee meals** (at cost)—If an operation feeds its employees, this number is part of its cost of food sold. In the case of a hotel, this could be a substantial amount considering the large numbers of housekeeping, front desk, maintenance, and food and beverage staff.

- **Comp** (at cost)—An abbreviation of the word "complimentary," this term is used to describe management giving a free meal to a guest. It could be because the guest was disgruntled, or merely because the person is prominent in the community and it is good for business to have this caliber of person in the establishment. Some operations comp public safety officers or persons on active military duty. Comps are subtracted from the cost of food sold.

- **Grease sales**—Old oil from the deep fryers, as well as fat or bones (if an operation does its own meat cutting) are sold to rendering companies. Since these items were a food cost originally, when they are sold the amount of the sale is taken as a credit to food cost.

- **Transfers to other units**—This type of transfer is used in larger operations in which there is more than one outlet for food. If one kitchen were to transfer goods to another kitchen, the loss would be subtracted from the food cost of the kitchen doing the transferring. The receiving kitchen would then add the transfer to its food cost.

- **Food to bar**—This is similar to transfers to other units but is used primarily where food items are transferred to the bar for use in drink preparation. Some examples are limes and strawberries, or food items such as cream, whipped cream, or olives. This should not be confused with a customer ordering and paying for food eaten in the bar.

Exhibit 2a

Food cost is directly affected not only by sales, but also by waste and theft.

Can you think of some other factors or circumstances that would add to an operation's food cost?

Calculating Food Cost

Fortunately, there is a formula for figuring food cost that takes into account the multiple purchases and uses of food items in a typical restaurant. To determine the value of the food that has been used, you must have both opening and closing inventory data. **Inventory** represents the dollar value of a food product in storage, and can be expressed in terms of units, values, or both. Most operations will have hundreds of food items in inventory at any given time. **Opening inventory** is the physical inventory at the beginning of a given period (such as the month of April). The **closing inventory** is the inventory at the end of a given period. It is important to remember that when one period ends, a new period begins. Therefore, the opening inventory is always equal to the closing inventory of the previous period. A period can consist of a day, week, month, quarter, or year. Most operations inventory and figure food cost monthly, but some quick-service operations, in particular, do it weekly. Rarely is it done on a daily, quarterly, or annual basis.

The formula for calculating food cost starts with adding the opening inventory plus **purchases,** which are all of the food purchases during that period. The total of these two numbers equals the **total food available,** or the dollar amount of all food available for sale. The closing inventory is then subtracted from the total food available, resulting in the *cost of food sold.* In the restaurant and foodservice industry, the terms *food cost* and *cost of food sold* are interchangeable.

This method is the only accurate way to obtain an actual food cost:

$$\left(\begin{array}{c} \textbf{Opening} \\ \textbf{inventory} \end{array} + \textbf{Purchases} = \begin{array}{c} \textbf{Total} \\ \textbf{food} \\ \textbf{available} \end{array} \right) - \begin{array}{c} \textbf{Closing} \\ \textbf{inventory} \end{array} = \begin{array}{c} \textbf{Cost of} \\ \textbf{food} \\ \textbf{sold} \end{array}$$

The calculation below shows how the food cost would be calculated if, for example, opening inventory was $1,000, purchases were $5,000, and closing inventory was $2,000. The food cost in this formula is expressed in dollars and cents.

$$\left(\$1,000 + \$5,000 = \$6,000 \right) - \$2,000 = \$4,000$$

Activity

Figuring Food Cost

Below are several problems in which you are to calculate missing information. Use the formula for determining food cost to calculate the missing amounts and complete the problems.

1. Opening inventory: $ 898
   Purchases: $ 4,782
   Closing inventory: $ 1,403

   What is the food cost? $_____

2. Opening inventory: $ 2,223
   Purchases: $ 14,764
   Food cost: $ 12,899

   What is the closing inventory? $_____

3. Purchases: $ 20,445
   Closing inventory: $ 2,112
   Food cost: $ 19,834

   What is the opening inventory for this period? $_____

   What is the opening inventory for the following period? $_____

4. If opening inventory is $8,375, food purchases are $18,249, and closing inventory is $6,997, what is the amount of total food available? $_____

   What is the food cost? $_____

5. If purchases are $12,665, closing inventory is $4,313, and total food available is $15,892, what is the opening inventory for this period? $_____

   What is the opening inventory for the following period? $_____

6. If opening inventory is $4,665, closing inventory is $3,998, and food cost is $20,441, what is the value of the total food available during the period? $_____

   What is the value of the food that was purchased during the period? $_____

Think About It...

Think About It...

What *should* a restaurant's food cost percentage be? In reality, different standards will apply depending on the operation, its type of service, location, and specific business goals. The "desired" food cost percentage does not hold true for all types of operations.

Calculating Food Cost Percentage

Now that the actual food cost has been determined, the next step is to calculate the food cost percentage. **Food cost percentage** is the relationship between sales and the cost spent on food to achieve those sales. Food cost percentage is often the standard against which food cost is judged. As with any measurement, food cost percentage is most often analyzed by comparing it to company standards, historical costs, or even industry standards. In most cases, the standard food cost percentage is a target determined by management. By expressing the cost of food sold in percentages, it can be compared on a month-to-month or week-to-week basis regardless of any fluctuation in sales. Controlling the food cost percentage becomes paramount if the operation is to be profitable.

To calculate food cost percentage, divide the food cost by sales as shown.

Food cost ÷ Sales = Food cost percentage

Thus, if food cost is $8,500, and sales are $27,490, the food cost percentage is 30.9 percent.

8,500 ÷ 27,490 = 0.309 *or* 30.9%

Exhibit 2b

Many operations use computers to automate calculations by menu item, menu category, or meal period.

*(To convert a decimal into a percentage, simply move the decimal two places to the right **or** multiply the answer by 100.)*

Another way to state this is to say that out of every dollar of sales, food cost accounted for about $0.31.

This example indicates an average food cost percentage for a given period. The calculation can be broken down into further levels of detail, such as by menu item, menu category, or meal period. *(See Exhibit 2b.)* For instance, the average breakfast food cost percentage might be lower than the average dinner food cost percentage.

Activity

How to Figure Food Cost Percentages

The following problems involve figuring food cost percentages. Problems 1–3 are related, so you may need to use some facts from one problem to complete another one. For a refresher on working with percentages, review the *Appendix* on basic mathematical operations beginning on p. 183.

1. Food cost: $ 5,722
   Sales: $18,900
   What is the food cost percentage? $ _____

   _____

   _____

   _____

   _____

2. Item cost: $ 1.35
   Selling price: $ 4.00
   Now what is the food cost percentage? $ _____

   _____

   _____

   _____

   _____

   _____

3. Server charges: $ 3.00
   Instead of: $ 4.00
   Now what is the food cost percentage? $ _____

   _____

   _____

   _____

   _____

   _____

How Costs and Sales Affect Food Cost Percentage

Food cost was identified as a variable expense in the previous chapter. This means it increases or decreases as sales increase or decrease and does so in direct proportion. That is, it *should* do so in direct proportion, if all of the standards and controls are followed. If the cost controls are not followed, it will not. Therefore, if an operation meets its standard food cost percentage month after month, its standards are set properly and the control system is working. If it does not meet its standard, then either the standards are set wrong or the controls are not working— or both.

For example, if a three-ounce hamburger has a food cost of $0.50 and sells for $1.50, the food cost percentage is 33.3 percent.

$0.50 ÷ $1.50 = 0.333 *or* **33.3%**

Assuming that this is the standard set by management, if the prep cook portions the hamburger at four ounces, thereby increasing the food cost to $0.60, the food cost percentage would increase to 40 percent.

$0.60 ÷ $1.50 = 0.40 *or* **40%**

The food cost percentage did *not* increase or decrease in direct proportion to the selling price because the standard was not met. Instead, the food cost increased, while the selling price stayed the same. In this case, the standard was set correctly. However, the control was not met, and the food cost percentage increased.

To look at it another way, assume that the server charged $2.00 for the hamburger, and it was made according to standard. The food cost percentage would be 25 percent.

$0.50 ÷ $2.00 = 0.25 *or* **25%**

At first glance, management might say that this is good because the food cost percentage is below the standard of 33.3 percent and more profit will be made. In the long run, however, this is *not* good, since the restaurant industry is very competitive. The customer will not pay $2.00 for an item that is only worth $1.50, especially if they could get it elsewhere for that amount. It is critical to remember that lost sales result in lost profit.

Exhibit 2c is another example. Rose either has not set her controls correctly or is not following them correctly. You can see from these examples how important it is that standards are met exactly. This task is one of the more difficult ones for management. There are a number of standards that must be met, and they must be monitored and controlled constantly.

Exhibit 2c

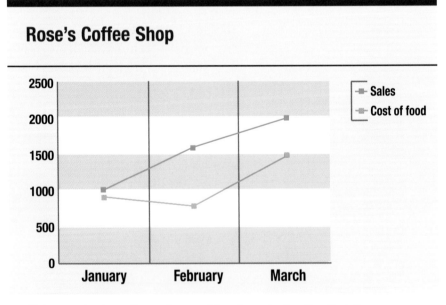

This graph show the sales and food costs for the first three months of this year for Rose's Coffee Shop. Notice that food cost is not in direct proportion to sales.

Summary

Many people, including some restaurant or foodservice managers, have a misconception that when food is purchased, it becomes food cost. This is not true. Food cost is the actual dollar value of the food used by an operation during a certain period. It includes the expense to an operation for costs incurred when food is consumed for any reason. Food cost includes the cost of food sold, given away, wasted, or even stolen. Some operations will further refine cost of food sold to get a more accurate number of how all the food is being used.

Fortunately, there is a formula for figuring food cost that takes into account the multiple purchases and uses of food items in a typical restaurant. To determine the value of the food that has been used, you must have both opening and closing inventory data. The formula for calculating food cost starts with adding the opening inventory plus purchases, which is all of the food purchased during that period. The total of these two numbers equals the total food available, or the dollar amount of all food available for sale. The closing inventory is then subtracted from the total food available. This results in the cost of food sold. Most operations inventory and figure food cost monthly, but some quick-service operations conduct inventory on a weekly basis.

Food cost percentage is the relationship between sales and the cost spent on food to achieve those sales. Food cost percentage is often the standard against which food cost is judged. As with any measurement, food cost percentage is most often analyzed by comparing it to company standards, historical costs, or even industry standards. Consistently meeting food cost percentage standards is one of the most difficult tasks for management.

Review Your Learning

1. **Which of the following are involved in figuring food cost?**

   A. Food purchases

   B. Food inventory

   C. Both A and B

   D. Neither A nor B

2. **Opening inventory is**

   A. figured and calculated periodically.

   B. the same as closing inventory of the previous period.

   C. Both A and B

   D. Neither A nor B

3. **Inventory in most foodservice operations is taken**

   A. annually and quarterly.

   B. quarterly or monthly.

   C. monthly or weekly.

   D. daily and weekly.

4. **When taking inventory,**

   A. opening inventory is counted, priced, and totaled.

   B. closing inventory is counted, priced, and totaled.

   C. Both A and B

   D. Neither A nor B

5. **Given the following data, determine the food cost percentage:**

   Opening inventory = $ 3,890
   Total food available = $ 74,381
   Closing inventory   = $ 2,996
   Sales   = $233,479

   A. 32.2%

   B. 31.1%

   C. 32.7%

   D. 30.6%

6. **If a chocolate éclair costs $0.45 to produce and the menu selling price is $1.75, but the server sells it for $1.00, the actual food cost percentage is**

   A. 25.7%.

   B. 38.9%.

   C. 45.0%.

   D. 22.2%.

7. **In the above problem, the standard food cost percentage for the éclair should be**

   A. 25.7%.

   B. 38.9%.

   C. 45.0%.

   D. 22.2%.

Using Standardized Recipes to Determine Standard Portion Cost

3

Inside This Chapter

- What Is a Standardized Recipe?
- Determining Standard Portion Cost

After completing this chapter, you should be able to:

- Explain why a standardized recipe is important to cost control and product consistency.
- Describe the information included in a standardized recipe.
- Compare "as purchased" and "edible portion" methods of determining the cost of recipe ingredients.
- Develop a recipe cost card using a standardized recipe.

Test Your Knowledge

1 **True or False:** If the standard portion size is four ounces, it means that five ounces should not be served because the operation would lose money, but it would be acceptable to serve three ounces. *(See p. 31.)*

2 **True or False:** A standardized recipe is the link between the menu description and the customer's expectation of the item. *(See pp. 28–29.)*

3 **True or False:** If the first ingredient in a standardized recipe is stated in AP format, then the entire recipe should be written using the AP method. *(See p. 31.)*

4 **True or False:** Recipe cost cards are based on standardized recipes. *(See p. 33.)*

5 **True or False:** There should be a recipe cost card for every multiple-ingredient item listed on the menu. *(See p. 33.)*

Key Terms

As purchased (AP) method

Butcher test

Conversion chart

Cooking loss test

Edible portion (EP) method

Portion size

Recipe cost card

Shrinkage

Standard portion cost

Standardized recipe

Introduction

One adage in the restaurant business is, "Everything starts with the menu." This is particularly true in the case of controlling food costs. In any well-run operation, menu offerings are based on the operation's standards, and staff are expected to meet those standards. If standards are not met, the restaurant will not be profitable.

The menu communicates an operation's standards to customers. What is stated on the menu is what the customer expects to get. For example, if the menu lists a twelve-ounce, charcoal-grilled choice rib eye steak, then the purchaser must purchase USDA choice rib eye, the prep cook or butcher must cut the rib eye into twelve-ounce portions, and the line cook must charcoal-grill it. In other words, the control mechanisms are set in place to ensure that a customer gets what has been described.

Exhibit 3a

Example of a Standardized Recipe

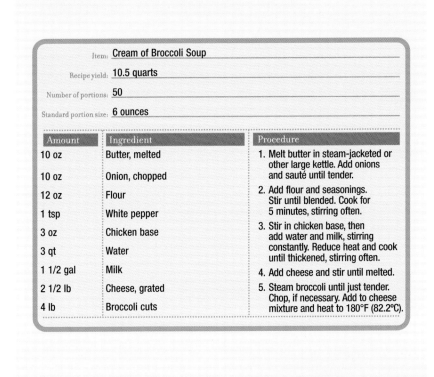

Amount	Ingredient	Procedure

Item: Cream of Broccoli Soup
Recipe yield: 10.5 quarts
Number of portions: 50
Standard portion size: 6 ounces

Amount	Ingredient
10 oz	Butter, melted
10 oz	Onion, chopped
12 oz	Flour
1 tsp	White pepper
3 oz	Chicken base
3 qt	Water
1 1/2 gal	Milk
2 1/2 lb	Cheese, grated
4 lb	Broccoli cuts

Procedure
1. Melt butter in steam-jacketed or other large kettle. Add onions and sauté until tender.
2. Add flour and seasonings. Stir until blended. Cook for 5 minutes, stirring often.
3. Stir in chicken base, then add water and milk, stirring constantly. Reduce heat and cook until thickened, stirring often.
4. Add cheese and stir until melted.
5. Steam broccoli until just tender. Chop, if necessary. Add to cheese mixture and heat to 180°F (82.2°C).

What Is a Standardized Recipe?

Each item listed on the menu should have its own standardized recipe. The standardized recipe is one of the key tools used in the control process. **Standardized recipes** list the ingredients and quantities needed for a menu item, as well as the methods used to produce it and its appropriate portion size. Standardized recipes are written in consistent language that refers to uniform production elements, so employees can exactly reproduce these recipes as needed. (See *Exhibit 3a.*) Other things included in a standardized recipe are:

- **Ingredient details**—Grades and brands of products needed, precise descriptions, etc.

- **Correct weights and measures of the ingredients**

- **Equipment and tools needed**—Specifies everything from pots to utensils—information that is particularly important to kitchen workers. Consider the difference between a spatula needed to turn one portion of fish (6″ spatula) and one needed to turn 150 pieces (16″ offset fish spatula).

- **Volume to be produced**—This depends partly on **portion size,** or the size of an item's individual serving, such as "four ounces of chicken."

- **Time required to make the item**

- **Storage and preparation information**—Includes information on thawing, what types of cuts need to be made, etc.

- **Cooking methods to be used**—Examples include blanching, sautéing, deep-frying, etc.

The more information you can give to employees, the more likely they will repeatedly produce the item correctly. A standardized recipe avoids the creative or personal preference approach to producing menu items. No one in the operation should include personal preferences in standardized recipes, nor should anyone be allowed to substitute amounts, ingredients, or cooking techniques.

Any deviation from the standardized recipe results not only in different levels of quality, but also in inaccurate costs being figured for that item and, consequently, an incorrect selling price. For example, if a recipe calls for 2 percent milk, heavy cream should not be used. Heavy cream might improve the recipe, but management has determined that the standardized recipe represents the quality level that they want. On the other hand, if management experimented with the recipe and decided that heavy cream was indeed a desirable improvement, the standardized recipe could be changed to reflect this fact. After this point, the revised standardized recipe should include the use of heavy cream.

Determining Standard Portion Cost

One of the most important reasons for using standardized recipes is to determine how much each serving costs to produce. The selling price for each menu item is directly related to preparation costs. Without a standardized recipe, a manager cannot arrive at an accurate standard portion cost for each item. **Standard portion cost** is the exact amount that one serving, or portion, of a food item should cost when prepared according to the item's standardized recipe.

The Two Methods of Costing Ingredients— AP and EP

There are two methods used to determine the cost of ingredients in a standardized recipe. These two methods are the AP method, which means "as purchased," and the EP method, which stands for "edible portion." There is a large difference between these two methods that affects both the quality of the recipe and the costs of the ingredients.

The **as purchased (AP) method** is used to cost an ingredient at the purchase price prior to any trim or waste being taken into account. In the AP method, all ingredient quantities are listed on the standardized recipe in the form in which they are purchased.

"Ten pounds of onion, diced" is an example of AP, as the recipe is calling for ten pounds of onion, as purchased. In this case, the chef would start with ten pounds of whole onion, peel and dice it, and

Think About It…

The EP method, in spite of being more time-consuming for figuring costs, is more exact. For example, if you gave several cooks an onion to peel, some would remove the skin only and some would remove the skin along with one or two layers of the onion. Thus, while everyone started out with the same amount, the yield in each case would be different.

add the onion to the recipe. The manager would calculate the cost of ten pounds of onion using the AP method.

Many fruit, vegetable, meat, poultry, and seafood items lose volume, and consequently weight, when cooked. Many times this is referred to as **shrinkage,** which is simply the amount of loss incurred when a product is trimmed and cooked or roasted. The **edible portion (EP) method** is used to cost an ingredient *after* it has been trimmed and waste has been removed so that only the usable portion of the item is reflected. Using the EP method to cost an ingredient, the quantity is listed on the standardized recipe using only the edible portion of that particular ingredient. For example, "ten pounds of diced onion" involves taking some quantity of onion, and then peeling, dicing, and weighing the results until there are ten pounds of peeled, diced onion. This ingredient would be costed using the EP method because the recipe is based on the edible portion of the onion only. To obtain a cost in this case, the original weight of the product would have to be used. So if you started with eleven pounds of onion in order to obtain ten pounds EP of diced onion, you would use the cost for eleven pounds to determine the cost of the onion used in the recipe.

It is imperative for a manager to know whether to use the AP method or the EP method to determine the costs of the ingredients in a standardized recipe. If the AP method is used to determine costs, but the recipe is actually written following the EP method, the selling price will be incorrect. The same will be true if the recipe is written using the AP method and the manager uses the EP method to determine the ingredient costs.

Unfortunately, most recipes do not come with the headings AP or EP. It is up to management to decide how to cost them. Normally there are clues in the directions of the recipes themselves. To further confuse the issue, quite often one recipe has both AP and EP directions mixed within it; one ingredient is listed as AP and the next ingredient is listed as EP. For example, the standardized recipe could list an ingredient either way, as shown in *Exhibit 3b.*

Exhibit 3b

Comparison of EP and AP Methods

10 lb onion, diced

10 lb diced onion = 11 lb onion with skin on

Determining AP Amounts from EP Amounts

In order to determine the AP quantity that is needed to result in a given EP quantity, you must know the cooking loss for the item. Many quantity cookbooks, purchasing textbooks, and yield books include charts of average cooking loss for common food items. A **conversion chart** is a list of food items showing the expected, or average, shrinkage from AP amount to EP amount. These charts are tools that a manager can use, and they work well in most cases. However, it is wise to conduct your own tests periodically to get the exact AP amount for your operation. A **butcher test** is used to measure the amount of shrinkage that occurs during the trimming of a meat product. This trimming includes deboning and removing fat and gristle. A **cooking loss test** is a way to measure the amount of product shrinkage during the cooking or roasting process. The amount of shrinkage due to trimming and cooking is usually expressed in terms of a percentage.

These tests are particularly important if the product is a high-cost item and if it is a product sold in high volume at the operation. If these two things are true, the item has a profound effect on the operation's food cost percentage and should not be left to chance. For example, if prime rib is a house specialty, a conversion chart might not be accurate because there are many variables that determine the amount of shrinkage, such as the length of time the product is cooked and at what temperature.

Activity

Calculating the Shrinkage of Prime Rib

Complete the chart below given the following information about the prime rib.

AP price per pound = $3.49	Final weight = 13 lb
EP price per pound = $4.54	Portion size = 12 oz
AP weight = 18 lb	

Shrinkage Calculation Chart					
Item:		Date:		Tested by:	
AP price per pound:					
EP price per pound:					
AP weight:	× AP price per pound:		AP net price:		
Final weight:	Final cost per pound:				
Shrinkage pounds:					
Shrinkage %:					

What is the cost per portion for the prime rib? _____

Creating Recipe Cost Cards

A key control in getting the proper relationship between a menu item's cost and its selling price is through the use of a recipe cost card. A **recipe cost card** is a tool used to calculate standard portion cost for a menu item. It is a table of ingredient costs for each item in the standardized recipe. If recipe cost cards are not used, the selling price is nothing more than a guess. It is essential that managers understand and use recipe cost cards since they are critical to the accurate figuring of selling prices. Several methods for determining menu prices will be discussed in greater detail in Chapter 4.

As with the standardized recipe, there should be a recipe cost card for every multiple-ingredient item listed on the menu. To properly fill out a recipe cost card and figure an item's standard portion cost, follow these steps:

1. Copy the ingredients from the standardized recipe to the recipe cost card. All ingredients should be recorded. The ingredients listed on the recipe cost card should match exactly the ingredients listed on the standardized recipe card.

2. List in the appropriate columns the amount and unit used for each ingredient needed to prepare the recipe.

3. From the invoice(s), list the cost of each ingredient as well as the unit listed on the invoice. Note: *The unit called for in the recipe is quite often different from the unit listed on the invoice.* For example, a recipe unit could be in pints, although that particular ingredient item was purchased in gallons. More often than not, the recipe unit and the invoice unit will not agree. The invoice unit will then need to be converted to agree with the recipe unit.

4. Convert the invoice unit to the unit used for the recipe in the recipe column, and figure the cost per recipe unit. As mentioned, if the invoice unit is gallons and the recipe unit is pints, convert the gallon cost into cost per pint and record this number on the cost card.

5. In the last column, figure the extended cost by multiplying the number of units needed for the recipe by the cost per recipe unit.

6. Add the cost of all ingredients together in the extension column. This gives you the total cost for preparing the entire recipe.

7. Divide the total cost by the number of portions the recipe will produce to get the standard portion cost.

Refer to *Exhibit 3c* and *Exhibit 3d* as you read the following steps to set up a recipe cost card for pasta sauce based on its standardized recipe.

Exhibit 3c

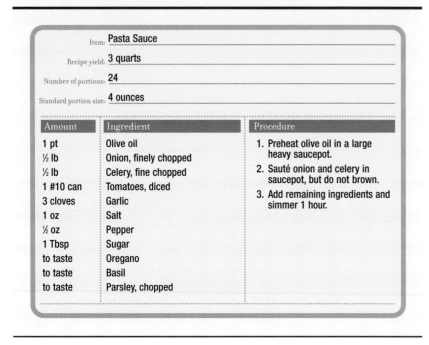

Standardized Recipe for Pasta Sauce

Item: Pasta Sauce

Recipe yield: 3 quarts

Number of portions: 24

Standard portion size: 4 ounces

Amount	Ingredient	Procedure
1 pt	Olive oil	1. Preheat olive oil in a large heavy saucepot.
½ lb	Onion, finely chopped	
½ lb	Celery, fine chopped	2. Sauté onion and celery in saucepot, but do not brown.
1 #10 can	Tomatoes, diced	
3 cloves	Garlic	3. Add remaining ingredients and simmer 1 hour.
1 oz	Salt	
½ oz	Pepper	
1 Tbsp	Sugar	
to taste	Oregano	
to taste	Basil	
to taste	Parsley, chopped	

1 Copy the ingredients from the standardized recipe to the **third column** of the recipe cost card.

2 List the amount and unit used for each ingredient in the appropriate column. For example, the first ingredient is olive oil, which is listed in the third column. In the first and second columns of the first row, put the amount and unit of the olive oil, i.e. 1 pint. The next ingredient is chopped onion, and the amount and unit is 0.5 (½) pound, which goes into the first and second columns respectively. Repeat this for the entire recipe as shown.

3 Next, look up the price for each ingredient on the invoice. Put the price and unit from the invoice in the fourth and fifth columns respectively.

4 The **recipe cost column** is calculated next. In the case of the first ingredient, olive oil, the recipe unit is pints, but the invoice unit is 4 gallons. This is typical of oils since they are commonly packed 4 gallons to the case. There are several ways this number can be converted. The easiest is to divide the cost of the case, $112.00, by 32 (the number of pints in 4 gallons) to arrive at $3.50. A slower way, but just as accurate, is to take the cost of the case, $112.00, and divide by 4 (4 gallons in a case) to get the cost of a gallon, $28.00. Then divide by 4 (4 quarts to a gallon) to get the cost per quart, $7.00. Then divide by 2 (2 pints in a quart) to get the cost per pint, $3.50.

5 Since the recipe calls for only 1 pint, the $3.50 is placed in the **extended cost column.** The second ingredient, onion, comes in 50-pound sacks. A half pound is needed. A 50-pound sack costs $16.50. Divide $16.50 by 100 (the number of half pounds in 50 pounds) to get 0.165, which is rounded to 0.17. Another method would be to divide $16.50 by 50 to get a price per pound of $0.33 and then divide by 2 to get a price for a half of a pound, $0.165

Exhibit 3d

Recipe Cost Card for Pasta Sauce Standardized Recipe

Item: **Pasta Sauce**

Recipe Amount	Recipe Unit	Ingredients	Invoice Cost	Invoice Unit	Recipe Cost	Recipe Unit	Extended Cost
2	**2**	**1**	**3**	**3**	**4**	**4**	**5**
1	pt	Olive oil	$ 112.00	4 gal	$ 3.50	pt	$ 3.50
0.5	lb	Onion, finely chopped	16.50	50 lb	.33	lb	0.17
0.5	lb	Celery, finely chopped	27.85	30 lb	.93	lb	0.46
1 can	#10	Tomatoes, diced	18.00	6/ #10	3.00	#10	3.00
3	Cloves	Garlic	0.05	clove	.05	clove	0.15
1	oz	Salt			.10		0.10
0.5	oz	Pepper			.10		0.10
1	tbsp	Sugar			.10		0.10
to taste		Oregano			.10		0.10
to taste		Basil			.10		0.10
to taste		Parsley, chopped			.10		0.10
					Total	**6**	$ 7.88
					# portions		24
					Cost/portion	**7**	$ 0.33

or $0.17. The 0.17 is placed in the extended cost column. (For this ingredient, the AP price was used because the recipe called for a half pound of onion, chopped. If it had called for a half pound of chopped onion, the EP method would have been used.)

Celery comes 30 pounds to the case. A half pound AP is needed. The case costs $27.85, which divided by 30 equals $0.93 per pound, and divided by 2 equals $0.46.

Diced tomatoes are packed 6 #10 cans per case. One can is needed. A case costs $18.00, which divided by 6 (cans per case) equals $3.00 per can.

The salt, pepper, and sugar are small amounts. In this case, a cost of $0.10 each is assigned.

The last three items are also assigned a cost of $0.10 each as the amount used is infinitesimal and not worth the time to calculate.

6 Next, add the numbers in the last column to get the **total cost of the recipe,** which is $7.88.

7 Finally, take the total cost ($7.88) and divide by the number of portions that the recipe will make (24) to get the **standard portion cost** for pasta sauce, which is $0.33.

Updating Recipe Cost Cards

Because of cost changes, it is imperative that recipe cost cards be updated periodically. The reason is, if a cost goes up and the selling price is not adjusted accordingly, the standard food cost percentage will not be met and the profit of the restaurant will be reduced. While this seems like a lot of work, once the initial setup of the cards is complete, they are quite easy to maintain.

Ingredient costs vary from area to area and, in many cases, change from day to day. This is usually true of meat, seafood, and produce, particularly if one or more of the ingredients is a high-cost item, and even more so if it is a recipe for a high-selling item. Recipe cost cards for these items should be reviewed weekly. Other recipe cost cards that are made up primarily of low-cost and consistently priced goods should be reviewed monthly.

Handling Customer Substitutions and Additions

In addition to creating recipe cost cards for each menu item, management will need to determine how to account for food costs when customers ask for substitutions or additions to standard menu items. Suppose, for example, that your establishment offers Fettuccini Alfredo as a standard menu item. How will you account for the cost when a customer requests that chicken breast be added to the dish? Or, how will you account for food cost if a customer requests that the mashed potato accompaniment be replaced with a more expensive vegetable? In the case of Fettuccini Alfredo, management might create a standardized recipe and cost card for the standard menu item and another standardized recipe and cost card for the Fettuccini Alfredo with chicken. Another possibility is to create a cost card for the substituted ingredient only. Regardless of how it is done, the important point is to account for the cost so that the operation maintains its standard food cost and desired profit.

Think About It...

Controlling food costs and maintaining profitable and competitive selling prices used to be an art, but computer software has made it an exact science. What strategies would you use to influence your management to purchase this type of software?

Recipe Cost Card Software

While figuring recipe cost card information is time consuming, its importance is indisputable. In this age of technology, a recipe cost card can be set up on any spreadsheet program. A variety of computer programs can also calculate the standard cost of a menu item. By inputting information similar to that in the example card, the programs can determine the standard portion costs. These programs can save time and labor compared to manual methods.

More and more restaurants, especially the larger ones and the chains, are moving toward automating many of these processes. There are literally scores of software programs available that will produce recipe cost cards. Some of the more sophisticated programs will make automatic adjustments. When an ingredient is purchased, received, and the invoice put into the system, the price of that ingredient will be adjusted on the recipe cost card. When the standard portion cost of the recipe reaches a predetermined level, the software will notify the manager that the cost of an item and the selling price are no longer in accord and that the standard food cost percentage is in jeopardy. Management can then take action to correct the problem.

Activity

Converting a Standardized Recipe to a Recipe Cost Card

Take the following standardized recipe for braised celery and create a recipe cost card for it. Remember to check your unit conversions between the invoice and the recipe.

Use the empty recipe cost card below to fill in the necessary information. The invoice costs for these ingredients have been provided.

Item:	Braised Celery
Recipe yield:	2.25 quarts
Number of portions:	24
Standard portion size:	3 ounces

Amount	Ingredient	Procedure
6 lb	Celery	1. Clean and trim the celery to 3-inch lengths.
4 oz	Butter	2. Sauté the celery in the butter, but do not brown.
3 pt	Chicken stock	3. Add the chicken stock and bring to a boil.
to taste	Salt	4. Cover and braise in the oven at 350°F (177°C) until tender, approximately one hour.
to taste	Pepper	5. Salt and pepper to taste.

Item: **Braised Celery Recipe Cost Card**

Recipe Amount	Recipe Unit	Ingredients	Invoice Cost	Invoice Unit	Recipe Cost	Recipe Unit	Extended Cost
		Celery	28.75	30 lb			
		Butter	50.40	24 lb			
		Chicken stock	3.00	1 gal			
		Salt			.10		
		Pepper			.10		
						Total	
						# portions	
						Cost/portion	

Summary

In any well-run operation, menu offerings are based on the operation's standards, and staff are expected to meet those standards. If standards are not met, the restaurant will not be profitable. The menu communicates an operation's standards to customers. What is stated on the menu is what the customer expects to get.

The standardized recipe is one of the key tools used in the control process. A standardized recipe is a written format used for consistently preparing and serving a given menu item. It includes a complete list of ingredients, their quantities, and the procedures to be followed each time that recipe is produced. Since a standardized recipe is so important, it must be clearly written and very detailed so that different cooks using the recipe will produce an identical product time after time.

Simply having standardized recipes in an operation is not enough— managers must ensure that all standardized recipes are followed and consistently prepared over time. Any deviation from the standardized recipe results not only in different levels of quality, but also in inaccurate costs being figured for that item and, consequently, an incorrect selling price.

One of the most important reasons for using standardized recipes is to determine how much each serving costs to produce. There are two methods used to determine the cost of ingredients in a standardized recipe. The as purchased (AP) method is used to cost an ingredient at the purchase price prior to any trim or waste being taken into account. The edible portion (EP) method is used to cost an ingredient after it has been trimmed and the waste has been removed to reflect only the usable portion of that item. There is a large difference between these two methods that affects both the quality of the recipe and the costs. It is imperative for a manager to know which method to use when determining the cost of ingredients in a standardized recipe.

Because of cost changes, recipe cost cards should be updated periodically. The reason is, if a cost goes up and the selling price is not adjusted accordingly, the standard food cost percentage will not be met, and the profit of the restaurant will be reduced.

Various computer programs are available for finding the standard cost of a menu item. More and more restaurants, especially the larger ones and the chains, are moving toward automating many of these processes. There are literally scores of software programs available that will produce recipe cost cards.

Review Your Learning

1 Standardized recipes are important for

A. consistency.

B. cost control.

C. customer satisfaction.

D. A, B, and C

2 Standardized recipes list the

A. total yield of the recipe.

B. number of portions the recipe yields.

C. Both A and B

D. Neither A nor B

3 A standardized recipe does *not* include the

A. names of ingredients.

B. amounts of ingredients.

C. quality level of key ingredients.

D. cost of the recipe.

4 An item that has been trimmed of all waste and is ready for use is known as

A. AP.

B. EP.

C. AT.

D. TW.

5 Which of these ingredients is listed as EP?

A. Two lb. browned ground beef

B. Two lb. ground beef, browned

C. Brown 2 lb. ground beef

D. None of the above

6 The objective of a recipe cost card is

A. to get an accurate standard portion cost.

B. to obtain a figure used in the determination of a selling price.

C. Both A and B

D. Neither A nor B

7 If a recipe calls for 9 ounces of cooking oil that costs $5.00 per quart, the cost of the oil on the recipe cost card would be

A. $0.31.

B. $1.41.

C. $1.88.

D. $2.82.

Notes

ss breast of chicken,
rooms and mozzarella cheese, ser
d of sauteed spinach $13.95

cken Parmesan
oneless, skinless chicken breast seasoned with
erbs, lightly breaded & pan-fried. Baked with
herb marinara sauce $13.95

Chicken Breast Ala Marsala
Boneless breast of chicken delicately seasoned
with herbs, sauteed with fresh mushrooms &
sweet marsala wine $13.95

Center Cut Pork Chops
Broiled to perfection. Served with applesauce
and herb roasted potatoes $13.95

Francisco's Pepper Steak
Beef tenderloin medallions sauteed in butt
with fresh mushrooms, sweet bell pepper
onions $14.50

mbo Fried Shrimp
d and deep-fried. Serve

Cost Control and the Menu—Determining Selling Prices and Product Mix

4

Inside This Chapter

- Determining Selling Prices for Menu Items
- Market Forces Affecting Selling Prices
- Menu Product Mix
- Monitoring Menu-Related Controls

After completing this chapter, you should be able to:

- Determine a selling price based on various markup methods.
- Explain how market forces affect menu prices.
- Explain how the menu product mix is used to determine the composite food cost of an operation's menu.
- Explain how the menu serves as a food cost control mechanism.

Test Your Knowledge

1 **True or False:** Price-value relationship refers to the customer's perceived worth of an item relative to its selling price. *(See p. 48.)*

2 **True or False:** The factor method for markups is identical to the last step of the TRA method. *(See p. 46.)*

3 **True or False:** The price-value relationship is a static formula to determine the worth of an item to the restaurant's customers. *(See p. 48.)*

4 **True or False:** Entrées and beverages are marked up by the same percentage. *(See p. 49.)*

5 **True or False:** A product mix reflects the composite food cost for a menu, taking into account the cost of the items, the selling prices, and the number sold. *(See p. 49.)*

Key Terms

Composite food cost
  percentage

Factor method

Markup

Markup differentiation

Markup on cost method

Menu engineering

Menu product mix

Price-value relationship

Pro forma income statement

Texas Restaurant Association
  (TRA) markup method

Introduction

The menu, its offerings, and its prices have a large influence on an operation's profit. In the restaurant business, the selling price of an item is based on its cost—not only food cost, but also labor and overhead costs to run the operation. Given this fact, the selling price must be adequate to cover all of the costs and result in some profit.

For a restaurant to be profitable, it must also sell its goods at the correct price from the customers' perspective. For example, if the selling price on the menu is set too high, sales will be lost. Lost sales mean lost profit. Conversely, if the selling price is set too low, profit will be lost because not enough is being charged for an item to offset all of its costs. Because of this, it is imperative for the restaurant to charge an amount that will allow a profit, but is not so high that it will turn away customers. At times, this can be a narrow price range in which to work.

Exhibit 4c

Calculating Markup Using the TRA Method (Part Two)

Step 1

Labor expenses	.32	
All other expenses	.29	(other controllable and noncontrollable costs, except food cost, added together)
Profit	.08	
Total	**.69**	

Step 2

1.00	
− .69	
.31	(divisor)

Step 3

$ 3.22	(menu item standard portion cost)
÷ .31	= $10.39 (menu selling price)

the selling price jump from $9.50 to $10.50, if the owners thought this was too severe a jump and would hurt sales, they would have to make a decision. If they did not take the full increase, another expense would have to be reduced or profit would suffer.

The Factor Method

The **factor method** is a popular formula used to determine menu prices based simply on the standard food cost percentage. The formula for the factor method is:

$$1.00 \div \text{Standard food cost percentage} = \text{Factor}$$

$$\text{Factor} \times \text{Menu item cost} = \text{Selling price}$$

Again, 1.00 is 100 percent, which represents sales or the menu item's selling price. If you took the information from the Slippery Noodle's pro forma income statement (see *Exhibit 4a*), and used the same item cost as in the previous calculation ($3.22), the formula would look like this:

$$1.00 \div .34 = 2.94 \qquad 2.94 \times 3.22 = \$9.47$$

In this case, the selling price would probably be rounded up to $9.50. Assuming that the standard food cost percentage for the operation across the board is 34 percent, the only step that needs to be taken to determine prices is to multiply each item's standard portion cost by the factor of 2.94 (a 34 percent food cost will always have a factor of 2.94, since 1.00 ÷ .34 = 2.94).

Markup on Cost Method

The third method is called the markup on cost method and is very popular within the foodservice industry. The **markup on cost method** is another simple formula used to determine a menu selling price based on the standard food cost percentage. The formula is:

$$\text{Menu item cost} \div \text{Standard food cost percentage} = \text{Selling price}$$

For example, using the Slippery Noodle's data again, the calculation would be:

$$\$3.22 \;\div\; .34 \;=\; \$9.47$$

Again, this figure would probably be rounded up to $9.50.

You are probably noticing a couple of patterns in these formulas. First, the result of the markup on cost method is the same as the result of the last step of the TRA method. Why would you want to go through all of the steps in the TRA method when all that is needed is the last step? The answer is that the TRA method takes into account all of the expenses and profit of the restaurant. If a cost line goes awry, corrections can be made in the formula to get profit back to where it should be. The only way to keep profit in line, at times, is to increase the selling price. The TRA method takes you through that process.

Another pattern that you should observe is that all the answers (except the one where the selling price was increased to offset a labor cost increase) are $9.47. Why? In reality, these are the same numbers, looked at in different ways. The fact remains that by using the same standards (budgeted sales, standard costs, profit) in each method, the resulting selling price is the same for each method. If a food cost of 34 percent is the standard, and the menu item standard portion cost is $3.22, no matter what method is used, the menu item must be sold at $9.47 to maintain a 34 percent food cost.

Activity

Using Formulas to Figure Menu Selling Prices

The following three problems will provide you with some practice in figuring menu selling prices. Each one asks you to use a different method. Read each problem and then calculate the menu selling price using the method suggested.

1. Using the *TRA method,* calculate the menu selling price for an item with a standard portion cost of $2.85. The profit equals 10 percent for the restaurant and labor expenses are currently at 30 percent, with all other expenses at 28 percent.

   Labor expenses: _____   Profit: _____

   All other expenses: _____   Total: _____

   Menu selling price: _____

2. Using the *factor method,* calculate the menu selling price for an item with a standard portion cost of $4.36. The standard food cost percentage is 34 percent.
   Menu selling price: _____

3. Using the *markup on cost method,* calculate the menu selling price for an item with a standard portion cost of $1.74. The standard food cost percentage is 34 percent.
   Menu selling price: _____

Market Forces Affecting Selling Prices

In the previous examples, the statement was made that the selling price on the menu would probably be $9.50 instead of $9.47. This would change the food cost percentage. In this case, it would be an infinitesimal change, but a change nevertheless. The selling price on the menu is not always the same price that is derived from one of the formulas. Alterations need to be made to menu selling prices primarily for three reasons (see *Exhibit 4d*):

1 Competition

2 Price-value relationship

3 Markup differentiation

Competition

Many customers purchase goods based solely on price. Sometimes, a competitor will force an operation to charge a lower price than intended. For example, quick-service establishments will often have "price wars" to compete for customers. To get customers to choose their operation, managers will match or beat a competitor's price.

This does not mean that the restaurant should arbitrarily charge at or below what a competitor charges. Management must first figure out what needs to be charged to meet the standard food cost percentage by completing a recipe cost card and calculating a markup.

Only when the selling price necessary to meet the standard has been determined can management make a rational decision regarding whether or not they want to meet, or beat, the competition's price on an item, or possibly not carry that item at all.

Exhibit 4d

Market Forces Affecting Selling Price

Competition

Selling price

Markup differentiation

Price-value relationship

Competitive pricing is prevalent in the quick-service segment of the industry. It is used to a lesser degree in the family dining segment and rarely in fine dining. The reason is that customers buying on the low end are more concerned with lower prices than with quality. Conversely, people purchasing on the high end are more concerned with quality and are less, if at all, concerned with price.

Not all competitive situations will force a lower price. After costing out an item, management may find that they can sell it at a higher price because the competition is selling at a higher price. Another reason for selling an item for a price higher than the standard markup could be that no one else in the market is selling the item. There are not many restaurants that can charge whatever price they want, however. In this case, management must price the item at what the market will bear.

Price-Value Relationship

The connection between the selling price of an item and its worth to the customer is known as the **price-value relationship.** In other words, customers must see value in an item before they will purchase it. How much they will pay depends on each item's perceived value to them. For example, if a customer is hungry for a hamburger, the hamburger has a value. If it is a small hamburger with onion, pickle, and mustard, it has a low value and therefore should have a low selling price. If it is a quarter-pound hamburger with lettuce and tomato added, it has a higher value and can command a higher price. If it is a half-pound hamburger served in a nice pub atmosphere, it has an even greater value. The customer will pay a certain price for the half-pound sandwich in a pub and consider it a good value, but would not be willing to pay the same price for the smaller hamburger when buying one in the drive-through lane. The customer would, however, pay a lesser price for the small hamburger and consider that purchase to have a good price-value relationship.

What makes this situation difficult is that the price-value relationship is not a static formula. A good value for one person may not necessarily be considered a good value by the next person. When pricing the menu, management needs to focus on the norm and ask, "Will the average customer perceive this as a good price value?" Much of the price-value relationship comes from competition, which affects the mindset of the customers as to what they are willing to pay for an item.

Exhibit 4e

Common Markup Percentages

Menu Item Category	Markup
Soups/ Appetizers	20–50%
Salads	30–45%
Entrées/ Sandwiches	25–50%
Desserts	20–50%
Beverages	5–30%

Markup Differentiation

Because of expectations in the market, different categories of food can get different markups. This is known as **markup differentiation**. Two extreme examples are beverages and steaks. A cup of coffee can be produced for less than $0.10 per cup and sold for $1.00, which is approximately a 10 percent food cost. If the same markup were used on a rib eye steak that costs $7.00, it would be sold at $70.00. Obviously, a restaurant would not sell very many steaks at that price. A rule of thumb that holds true, for the most part, is that the lower the cost, the higher the markup. While these are two lopsided examples, the point is that different categories on the menu bring different markup expectations and levels of tolerance from customers. *Exhibit 4e* shows the widely accepted markup percentages for different menu categories.

Menu Product Mix

By now, you know that in order for a foodservice operation to be profitable, the menu as a whole must produce a certain standard food cost percentage. So how do you measure the overall average food cost percentage when the menu includes some items that sell at lower or higher food cost percentages due to external market factors?

This average can be determined by looking carefully at the menu product mix. The **menu product mix** is a detailed analysis that shows the quantities sold of each menu item, along with their selling prices and standard portion costs. The menu product mix is used to determine the composite food cost percentage. The **composite food cost percentage** is the weighted average food cost percentage for all items sold. It is important to remember that you should not simply total the food cost percentage column and divide by the number of menu items. The result would not be accurate because these percentages are not weighted by the quantity of each item sold.

It is this average—not each individual item—that must meet the operation's standard food cost percentage. If this is true, then why bother figuring different markups for each item? The answer is that the menu product mix allows management to see how each individual item contributes to the overall sales and cost-effectiveness of the menu. The markup of each item on the menu tells management where that item stands in relationship to the overall product mix and the standard food cost percentage.

In the markup formula examples in the previous section of this chapter, the menu item's standard portion cost is $3.22, and it was determined that the item would have to sell for $9.47 to get a 34 percent food cost, which is the operation's standard. (It was also determined that the price would most likely be rounded to $9.50.) Assuming that the menu item is a rib eye steak sandwich and that the operation's management looked at the competition, considered the price-value relationship, and decided that the local market would only bear $9.00 for this item, the menu selling price would be set no higher than $9.00. Management now knows that for every rib eye steak sandwich sold, the operation needs to make up $0.47 to offset the fact that the item is priced below the standard food cost percentage. They must now look at other menu items to make up this difference.

The Menu Product Mix Spreadsheet

In order to identify how menu items contribute to the composite food cost percentage, managers use a simple chart or spreadsheet. On this spreadsheet, the number sold of each item is multiplied by the item's standard portion cost to get the total cost. Likewise, the number sold is multiplied by the selling price to get total sales. Total cost is then divided by total sales to get the product mix for this entire menu. The menu product mix spreadsheet shown in *Exhibit 4f* illustrates that each of the items sold has a different food cost percentage. In this case, the composite food cost percentage for the entire menu is 36 percent.

To further understand how this tool can be used, change the standard food cost for the restaurant to 35 percent. There are many ways to lower the food cost percentage, but assume that management wants to do it by increasing the selling prices of French fries and onion rings. By increasing the price of each serving of French fries or onion rings by $0.10, the results will change as shown in *Exhibit 4g*. The restaurant now has a composite food cost percentage of 35 percent and is therefore meeting its standard.

The examples in the section on product mix were created using a spreadsheet program. In addition, there are numerous software programs that analyze menu product mix as well as several different versions of menu engineering. **Menu engineering** is similar to analyzing the menu product mix, but additionally it takes into account an item's contribution margin (the difference between an item's selling price and its food cost) and its popularity.

Exhibit 4f

Menu Product Mix Spreadsheet

Item	Number Sold	Cost	Selling Price	Food Cost Percentage	Total Cost	Total Sales
Hamburger	250	$ .60	$ 1.50	40%	$ 150.00	$ 375.00
Hot dog	190	.37	1.00	37%	70.30	190.00
French fries	225	.42	.85	49%	94.50	191.25
Onion rings	157	.61	1.25	49%	95.77	196.25
Carbonated beverages	428	.15	.85	18%	64.20	363.80
Ice cream cone	118	.26	.75	35%	30.68	88.50
Total				**36%**	**$ 505.45**	**$ 1,404.80**

Exhibit 4g

Changing the Selling Price Affects Food Cost Percentage

Item	Number Sold	Cost	Selling Price	Food Cost Percentage	Total Cost	Total Sales
Hamburger	250	$ .60	$ 1.50	40%	$ 150.00	$ 375.00
Hot dog	190	.37	1.00	37%	70.30	190.00
French fries	225	.42	**.95**	44%	94.50	213.75
Onion rings	157	.61	**1.35**	45%	95.77	211.95
Carbonated beverages	428	.15	.85	18%	64.20	363.80
Ice cream cone	118	.26	.75	35%	30.68	88.50
Total				**35%**	**$ 505.45**	**$ 1,443.00**

Activity

Completing a Menu Product Mix

A partially complete menu product mix spreadsheet is shown below. Fill in the rest of the information, including the columns for food cost percentage, total cost, and total sales. Then calculate the composite food cost percentage for the menu.

Menu Product Mix Spreadsheet

Item	Number Sold	Cost	Selling Price	Food Cost Percentage	Total Cost	Total Sales
Vegetarian meat loaf	354	$ 1.23	$ 2.95			
Vegetable fried rice	487	.89	2.75			
Apple tofu sausage	525	.96	2.85			
Plantain chips	1,001	.36	1.25			
Beverages	1,156	.18	1.00			
Tofu ice cream	194	.22	.85			
Total						

Monitoring Menu-Related Controls

Now that you understand how pricing separate items affects the composite food cost percentage for the menu, the next step is to examine how managers can identify concerns directly related to food cost percentages. There are three factors, which should be examined and compared to each other:

1 Standard food cost percentage for the operation

2 Composite food cost percentage based on the menu product mix

3 Actual food cost percentage calculated from the income statement

If all three match, there are no apparent problems in the restaurant regarding food cost. If they do not match, this indicates problems that need to be investigated. The manner in which these factors do not match will give management insight into where the problem lies, and whether it is related to the menu or to the actual activities within the operation. In each method of determining what the cause might be, a manager must analyze the variances among these three factors.

Is the Menu the Problem?

To see if the problem is with the menu itself (such as the items listed on it or the prices at which the items are being sold), the composite food cost percentage should be compared with the operation's standard food cost percentage. The general steps to follow include:

1 Comparing the composite food cost percentage with the operation's standard food cost percentage.

2 Identifying any variance from the standard.

If the variance is equal to the difference between the standard or budgeted food cost and the actual food cost, as shown on the income statement, it will be necessary to adjust the menu pricing structure. (See *Exhibit 4h.*) Using the previous formulas in this chapter for standard food cost and product mix, assume that a restaurant's standard food cost percentage is 28 percent and the income statement calculation results in an actual percentage of 32 percent for the month. If management analyzed the menu product mix and found a composite food cost percentage of 32 percent, then management's only solution in this case is to adjust the items or prices on the menu to eliminate any future variance and bring the actual food cost percentage back down to 28 percent.

This is an extremely important concept to master. Many managers, particularly in chain operations where they have little control over menu pricing, have struggled to attain the company's standard food cost when there is no realistic way to do so. The product mix and the standard food cost must match if there is any expectation of achieving the standard on the income statement.

Exhibit 4h

Cost Variance and Menu Control

Standard food cost percentage − Composite food cost percentage = Variance

Standard food cost (on budget) − Actual food cost (on income statement) = Variance

Variance = Variance?

If these variances equal each other, then the problem of high food cost is in the menu pricing structure.

Possible solutions:

▪ Increase prices.

▪ Eliminate high-cost/low-selling items and replace with low-cost items that have higher sales potential.

▪ Evaluate portion sizes.

Assuming that management does have control of the menu, there are several solutions that can be explored to bring the menu into agreement with the standard. The first inclination would be to increase prices. Although this could certainly be a solution to the problem, it may not be the wisest choice. Care must be taken when increasing prices not to exceed the price-value relationship perceived by the customers. Another alternative would be to eliminate high-cost/low-selling items and replace them with low-cost items that have a higher sales potential. Low-cost items can also be marketed in such a way as to encourage the customer to choose them over higher-cost items. Another consideration would be to evaluate the portion sizes. However, as with increasing prices, management must be careful not to affect the price-value relationship by cutting portions to the extent of causing customer discontent.

Activity

Menu Controls and the Executive Chef

Find a partner in class and decide who will play the executive chef and who will play the production manager. Read the following scenario and take about five minutes to prepare for the conversation. If you are the executive chef, be attentive to what the production manager has to say and listen to the rationale. At the same time, think of reasons to argue that the production manager's points might not be correct. If you are the production manager, prepare a list of reasons along with a strong rationale for why you believe the solution lies with the menu needing adjustments. You might want to run some figures to support your rationale.

You are the production manager for Spaghetti Galore and More, a budget Italian eatery. It is part of a metropolitan chain with six units. The corporate executive chef, Connie Cosentino, is visiting your operation. As production manager, one of your responsibilities is to maintain the food cost at the company's standard. Connie tells you that your food cost has been out of line and she needs you to address it immediately. You tell her that you are also very concerned about the high cost, which is why you have run a menu product mix analysis. You have discovered that the composite food cost percentage is actually higher than the company standard by 4 percent. Therefore, the problem is in the menu pricing and not in your operation. Convince Connie that the menu needs to be changed to meet the company's standard food cost percentage.

After the role-play, debrief with the following questions:

1. What were the reasons given to look more carefully at the menu?

2. Do you think that the rationale supported this suggestion?

3. What could the production manager have done differently to influence the chef?

Is the Problem Operational?

Now consider a different scenario. In this case, the operation's composite food cost percentage as calculated through the menu product mix is equal to its standard food cost percentage, but, by comparing budget to the income statement, management has identified a variance between the standard food cost and the actual food cost. Under these circumstances the variance is usually caused by an operational problem within the restaurant.

For example, if the composite food cost percentage calculated through the menu product mix analysis is 35 percent, and it matches the restaurant's standard of 35 percent, but the actual food cost percentage calculated from data on the income statement is 40 percent, then the issue is not related to the menu. In theory, the operation should be able to achieve the standard food cost percentage based on its current menu offerings. The variance between these figures rests with one or more of the operational controls which will be discussed in detail in subsequent chapters.

Summary

The menu, its offerings, and its prices have a large influence on an operation's profit. For a restaurant to be profitable, it must also sell its goods at the correct price from the customers' perspective.

Restaurants use a variety of methods to calculate markup and determine selling prices. The Texas Restaurant Association (TRA) markup method best reflects the direct relationship between profit and selling price. It uses a formula for menu cost markups that takes into account the sales, costs, and profit. The factor method determines menu prices based simply on the standard food cost percentage. The markup on cost method is another formula used to determine a menu selling price based on the standard food cost percentage.

The selling price on the menu is not always the same price that is derived from one of the formulas. Menu selling prices might need to be altered for market-related reasons such as competition, customers' perceptions of the price-value relationship, and markup differentiation.

The menu product mix is a detailed analysis that shows the quantities sold of each menu item, their selling prices, and their standard portion costs. It is used to determine the composite food cost percentage for all items sold. It is this average—not each individual item—that must meet the operation's standard food cost percentage.

Activity

Burrito Biggies Menu Product Mix

You are the general manager of Burrito Biggies, a popular quick-service restaurant, and have been given this assignment.

1 Calculate the missing information and complete the menu product mix spreadsheet below.

2 What is the composite food cost percentage for Burrito Biggie's menu? _____

Menu Product Mix Spreadsheet

Item	Number Sold	Cost	Selling Price	Food Cost Percentage	Total Cost	Total Sales
Taco	890		$ 0.89	36%		$ 792.10
Burrito	775	$0.42		26%	$ 325.50	1,255.50
Tamale	800	0.29	0.79		232.00	
Chili con queso/chips	520		1.49	27%	208.00	774.80
Salsa/chips	780	0.26	0.89	29%		694.20
Beverages	1,650		0.89	18%	264.00	
Total					$	$

3 You have just found out that the cost of Cheddar and Monterey Jack cheese will be going up substantially due to a major strike by your dairy distributor's delivery personnel. You have refigured the recipe cost cards for the items using these ingredients and have come up with new costs: tacos at $0.35, burritos at $0.46, and chili con queso at $0.46. Butch Biggs, the owner of Burrito Biggies, will not stand for any increase in the standard food cost percentage, nor will he let you change the recipes or portion sizes. You are therefore limited to price increases.

Refigure the menu product mix information using the revised costs and determine what you will do to offset these increases.

NOTE: You are not limited to changing the selling price of those items that have an ingredient cost increase. You can change the selling price of anything on the menu.

Worksheet to reflect changes in the product mix:

Menu Product Mix Worksheet						
Item	Number Sold	Cost	Selling Price	Food Cost Percentage	Total Cost	Total Sales
Taco	890	$ 0.35				
Burrito	775	0.46				
Tamale	800	0.29			$ 232.00	
Chili con queso/chips	520	0.46				
Salsa/chips	780	0.26			202.80	
Beverages	1,650	0.16			264.00	
Total					$	$

4 Create a short presentation, including a new menu product mix analysis that you will give to Mr. Biggs regarding the cost increase on cheese. Your presentation should describe how you plan to offset the cost increase, while maintaining the operation's standard food cost percentage. You also want to reassure Mr. Biggs that customers will not be able to tell any difference in product quality or consistency.

5 Use the menu product mix spreadsheet below for your presentation. Be able to fully explain and justify your proposal.

Menu product mix spreadsheet for presentation to Mr. Biggs:

Menu Product Mix Spreadsheet						
Item	Number Sold	Cost	Selling Price	Food Cost Percentage	Total Cost	Total Sales
Taco	890	$ 0.35				
Burrito	775	0.46				
Tamale	800	0.29			$ 232.00	
Chili con queso/chips	520	0.46				
Salsa/chips	780	0.26			202.80	
Beverages	1,650	0.16			264.00	
Total					$	$

Review Your Learning

Use the following pro forma income statement data to answer questions 1–3:

Sales: $450,690

Cost of food sold: $110,575

Labor expenses: $125,989

All other expenses: $150,500

1 **A menu item's standard portion cost is $4.50. Using the TRA method, the item should be priced at**

A. $8.75.

B. $11.25.

C. $21.50.

D. None of the above.

2 **A menu item's standard portion cost is $1.90. Using the markup on cost method, the item should be priced at**

A. $5.32.

B. $7.60.

C. $9.00.

D. Cannot be determined from data given

3 **Using the factor method, the factor for the item in Question 2 would be**

A. 1.4.

B. 2.5.

C. 4.

D. 14.

4 **The TRA markup method differs from the factor and markup on cost methods by accounting for**

A. expenses and profit.

B. standard portion cost.

C. food cost percentage.

D. A and B only

5 **The final selling price on a menu is affected by**

A. competition.

B. standard food cost percentage.

C. price-value relationship.

D. All of the above

6 **A menu product mix is**

A. all of the ingredients that go into a standardized recipe.

B. an average of the number of items in each category on a menu.

C. the list of food items in inventory.

D. a composite food cost taking into account all items on the menu and their quantities sold.

7 **If the food cost on the income statement and the composite food cost are each 4 percent higher than the standard, then there is**

A. a problem with the menu.

B. a problem with the standard.

C. a recipe problem.

D. no problem.

Controlling Food Costs in Purchasing and Receiving

5

Inside This Chapter

- Purchasing Procedures and Cost Control
- Catering Purchases
- Butcher Test
- Receiving Procedures and Cost Control

After completing this chapter, you should be able to:

- Explain how a specification becomes a control in the purchasing function.
- Explain the parts of a purchase specification and of a purchase order.
- Explain various purchasing methods and their effects on the price of goods.
- Calculate a yield test that identifies the difference between AP price and EP cost.
- Identify factors that affect the purchase price.
- Distinguish between perishable and nonperishable goods and their relationship to the purchasing cycle.
- Calculate the par stock amount to order of a product.
- Calculate the amount to purchase, using EP amount and yield percent.
- Calculate the amount of goods to purchase for catered events.
- Calculate a butcher test, or meat yield test.
- Describe the proper procedures for receiving goods.

Test Your Knowledge

1   **True or False:** Foodservice buyers should purchase goods at the lowest possible price. *(See p. 69.)*

2   **True or False:** A specification is a communication link between the buyer and the supplier which tells the supplier exactly what the buyer wants. *(See pp. 63–64.)*

3   **True or False:** Prices quoted to the buyer by the supplier are quoted AP. *(See p. 69.)*

4   **True or False:** The responsibility for purchasing should be fixed, with only one person purchasing goods, or having one person delegated to purchase goods for a category. *(See p. 62.)*

5   **True or False:** When evaluating an item's cost, AP is more relevant than EP. *(See p. 71.)*

6   **True or False:** A butcher test and a meat yield test are virtually the same thing. *(See p. 79.)*

7   **True or False:** A specification includes product name, intended use, grade, product size, pack size, price, and general instructions to the bidders. *(See p. 63.)*

8   **True or False:** The standing order method of purchasing is used primarily with canned, frozen, and dry goods. *(See p. 66.)*

9   **True or False:** One-stop shop is a method of purchasing that means you must buy 100 percent of your groceries from one purveyor. *(See p. 68.)*

10 **True or False:** The cost-plus system of purchasing involves the restaurant purchasing goods from a supplier at the supplier's cost plus an agreed-upon percentage. *(See p. 68.)*

11 **True or False:** The commissary method of purchasing includes some manufacturing of premade goods according to the chain's specifications. *(See p. 69.)*

12 **True or False:** Par stock is the amount of product that is normally used between delivery dates, plus a safety factor. *(See p. 75.)*

Key Terms

As served (AS)

Butcher test

Buyer

Commissary

Competitive quotes

Cost-plus

Invoice

Market quotation sheet

Nonperishable goods

One-stop shop

Par stock

Perishable goods

Purchase order

Quotes

Sealed bid

Specification

Standing order

Yield chart

Yield percentage

Yield test

Introduction

Purchasing and receiving are two key areas in the control process of the restaurant and foodservice industry. When a customer orders an item from the menu, the customer expects to receive what the menu has listed. If size, shape, color, grade, or portions are mentioned, then those food characteristics are what the customer expects and what the customer should receive. The person responsible for purchasing the items for the restaurant or foodservice operation must recognize this customer expectation and procure exactly what is stated on the menu. (See *Exhibit 5a.*) This chapter introduces you to the purchasing process and various factors that need to be considered to ensure that your customers' food and menu expectations are met or exceeded. It will also present a variety of methods you can use in purchasing various products.

You will learn that in addition to buying the correct item, the correct amount must be acquired. If too many goods are purchased, not only is the restaurant's capital tied up in inventory, but if the goods are perishable, they might spoil. If too few goods are purchased, there is the danger of running out. Purchasing, like every other section in the restaurant or foodservice operation, is an area where costs can get out of line. Therefore, controls must be instituted to prevent this from happening.

You will learn how to determine pricing by looking at the AP and EP costs of items. You will also learn how to figure costs and amounts to purchase using such techniques as yield tests, par stock, and butcher tests. Catering purchases are unique since these are usually one-time events, and you will learn methods to assist you in determining the purchasing requirements for these situations.

Perishable and nonperishable food items also have unique attributes that need to be considered in the purchasing process. This chapter will review the factors that need to be considered to keep costs in control.

Finally, receiving is an area in many restaurant or foodservice operations that gets little, if any, consideration. This is an unfortunate situation because there are many ways for costs to increase in this procedure. In this chapter, you will learn that inaccurate deliveries and invoices, spoilage, and theft can all contribute to food cost deviating from the standard.

Buyers select the food needed to produce menu items that satisfy customers' expectations.

Purchasing Procedures and Cost Control

The first decision that needs to be made in purchasing is determining who will do it. It could be one of several persons depending on the size of the operation. In very large foodservice operations such as major hotels, hospitals, and college foodservices, a purchasing agent will do the buying. In smaller operations, it could be the general manager, production manager, or chef. Regardless of who does it, only one person should purchase any given item. This person is referred to as the **buyer** and is the sole person responsible for purchasing goods for an operation. Taking this approach eliminates any confusion regarding what was purchased and when. It also minimizes the risk of running out of a product or having too much of it on hand. For example, in a larger operation, the chef could purchase meat, seafood, and produce, while the sous chef could order dairy, baked goods, dry goods, and supplies. Although two people are purchasing, only one person is buying in each respective category.

While it is common for management to delegate purchasing, it is extremely important that the person selected to purchase products is trained and knowledgeable about the subject. As will be seen throughout this chapter, purchasing is not a haphazard chore. Some buyers purchase only the very finest. "Start out with quality, end up with quality" is their mantra. Other buyers "browbeat" the salesperson to get the lowest possible price. Both of these methods are foolhardy. A restaurant does not always need the finest or the best, and to rely solely on this strategy is wasting money. A salesperson who knows that the buyer is going to negotiate down will start with a higher price, drop it under pressure, and leave with the order. Only by following correct purchasing procedures and having controls set in place will the restaurant get the right item at the right price. Therefore, if management is going to delegate this responsibility, it must be passed on to someone who has been trained in the operation's purchasing procedure.

What to Purchase: The Specification

Because there is such a wide variety of food available, the specification is a major control device. Through the specification, management sets policy as to which brands, grades, and variety of food products will be ordered for the operation. A specification ties together what is written on the menu and what is called for on the standardized recipe. It also controls the purchasing and receiving procedures.

Exhibit 5b

Chocolate, nuts, caramel, and coconut are informal specifications for the candy you like to eat.

Specifications are probably nothing new to you. They are used in our lives on a daily basis. If you were to buy some clothes, you would have a specific size, preferred style, and color in mind. Even simple things like purchasing a candy bar have specifications—chocolate, caramel, nuts, cherries, all of these, some of these, or none of these. (See *Exhibit 5b*.) While the specifications in our daily lives are informal, the specifications used in the restaurant and foodservice industry are formal.

A **specification** is a document listing the product name, its intended use, grade, size, and other product characteristics. It also includes general instructions regarding delivery, payment procedures, and other pertinent data. Basically, it tells the supplier exactly what the buyer wants. For example, if a buyer were to order a case of apples from a produce company, the company could possibly ship any type of apple. Without a specification, the supplier would not know the variety, degree of ripeness, pack, size, and preferred growing region of the apples the buyer needs.

However, before a buyer can purchase any perishable or nonperishable food, management, with input from the chef or production manager, must write the specifications for the foods needed to produce the standardized recipes of the menu items. Large operations typically write formal specifications; smaller operations might use verbal specifications. A lengthy formal specification includes the following information, while a short informal specification includes only a limited amount of this information (see *Exhibit 5c*):

Exhibit 5c

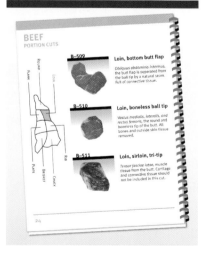

Specifications identify exactly what the buyer should purchase.

- **Product name**

- **Intended use**

- **Grade**—USDA, brand name, trade association endorsement

- **Product size**—Could include portion size; weight ranges for food items such as roasts, ribs, whole chickens, or whole fish; size of produce

- **Packaging**—Size of pack, type of packaging material

- **Product characteristics**—Color, amount of trim, type of preservation, degree of ripeness, point of origin
- **Acceptable substitutions; "or equal"**
- **General instructions to bidders**—Payment procedures, delivery requirements

A specification for meat would be greatly simplified by using *The Meat Buyers Guide,* published by The North American Meat Processors Association.

Once the specifications are written, they are circulated to possible suppliers to determine which suppliers will provide each product. Ultimately, specifications are used by the buyer, the receiving clerk, the kitchen, and accounting. Thus, specifications are a communication link, not only with the supplier, but also internally.

The Purchase Order

The purchase order is a primary control used throughout the purchasing, receiving, and accounts payable process. (See *Exhibit 5d.*) Without it, many things can, and usually do, go wrong. *Exhibit 5e* illustrates what can happen without the control of a purchase order. In this example, the buyer ordered 100 pounds of beef tenderloin at $9.50 per pound. The supplier shipped 200 pounds. The receiver, not knowing what the buyer ordered, signed for 200 pounds, which was the quantity on the invoice. Without a purchase order, accounting paid the supplier's invoice for 200 pounds of tenderloin at $11.00 per pound. What do you think happened to this operation's standard food cost this month?

Exhibit 5d

Sample Purchase Order

6023 W. Pratt Chicago, IL 60601 Phone: 773-555-5555		Hawaiian Dream Restaurant				PO: 56789-00
				Charge Account: 304-6395		
Date of Order: 11/16				**Ship to:** PO address		
Date Required: 11/23			**Price**	**Per**	**Amount**	
Quantity	**Unit**	**Item**	16.39	cs	49.17	
3	cs	Pineapple chunks, fancy	18.62	cs	55.86	
3	cs	Pineapple slice mini, fancy heavy syrup				

Purchaser signature _____   Manager signature_____

Using a purchase order for every order that the buyer places can prevent the lack of control illustrated by the example shown. A **purchase order** is a form listing the products to be purchased, their price, delivery date, and other important information. It includes the following features:

- Unique number to identify the purchase order

- Name of the ordering restaurant or foodservice operation, its address, and its phone number

- Date of the order

- Signature of the person placing the order

- Supplier's name, address, phone number, and contact name

- Date of delivery, terms of payment, and any special instructions

- Each item to be purchased, the quantity and unit of the item, the item's unit cost, and the extended cost of the item

- Total cost of the order

Exhibit 5e

Problems with Lack of Purchasing Control

100 lb of beef tenderloin are wasted.

Buyer orders 100 lb of beef tenderloin at $9.50/lb.

Shipper sends 200 lb of beef tenderloin.

Receiver signs for 200 lb, which is on invoice at $11.00/lb.

Accountant pays $11.00/lb instead of $9.50/lb.

After creating a purchase order for the needed items, the buyer sends the purchase order to the supplier and a copy to the receiving clerk. The receiving clerk receives the items, notes on the purchase order what the supplier has sent, and forwards the purchase order to accounting. Accounting then compares the purchase order to the supplier's **invoice**, a bill that accompanies the delivery of goods, to determine the correct amount to pay the supplier. By using a purchase order, everyone knows what has been purchased, at what price, when to expect it to be delivered, and when payment is due. Unless one person with an excellent memory does the purchasing, receiving, and bill paying, a purchase order is a mandatory control in every restaurant and foodservice operation.

How to Purchase

Once you know what you want to purchase, then you need to know how to purchase those items. There are various ways to purchase products, and some are more economical than others, thus contributing to a lower food cost. On the other hand, some are misused and end up costing the restaurant or foodservice organization. Most restaurant or foodservice organizations will use one or more of the following methods in their purchasing process. See *Exhibit 5f* for a comparison of the most common purchasing methods.

Exhibit 5f

Purchasing Methods Comparison

	Competitive Quotes	Standing Order	One-Stop Shop	Cost-Plus	Sealed Bids	Commissary
Primary use	Independent restaurants, smaller operations	Bakery, coffee, dairy products	Independents and chains	Chain operations	Large foodservice units such as schools, hospitals, government	Chains and franchised operations
Requirements	Detailed specs	Par stock; must show manager what is removed and brought in	Restaurant specs; par stock	Purchase 100% of product line from one purveyor	Amount needed for a period of time, usually a year	Paper supplies printed with company logo; purchase 100% of supplies
Pros	Lowest price	Keeps stock levels even	Delivery costs reduced with one truck stopping; purchasing online	Lowest possible price	Lowest bid	Efficient; customized supplies
Cons	Lack of specs could lead to lesser-value shipments	Abuse by delivery person; food cost goes up	If supplier is out of item, no backup purveyor; supplier may not offer lowest prices	No competition between bidders	Delivery times need to be negotiated	Often owned by parent company of restaurant chain; conflict of interest

■ **Competitive quotes**—This is a common purchasing method used by independent restaurants and smaller operations. The buyer completes a **market quotation sheet** with the items and item specifications that the operation needs. This sheet is a standardized form that is given to two or more suppliers who are then asked to provide a price quote for the items needed. The **quotes,** which are the prices cited by a purveyor for a specific product, are analyzed, and the order is then placed with the chosen supplier. For this method to be successful, specifications must be established. If they are not, then anything could be shipped and not necessarily be the best value for the restaurant or foodservice operation. If specifications are used, then the lowest price would be the best value, as all suppliers are bidding on an identical product.

■ **Standing order**—This method is used primarily for bakery, coffee, and dairy products. In this method the restaurant or foodservice operation establishes a par stock for each item. A **par stock** is the level that must be continually in stock from one delivery to the next. To determine a par stock level follow these steps:

1. Determine the amount of time between deliveries (i.e. weekly, bimonthly, or monthly).

2. Determine the estimated amount used during this period. This should be done for each item in the storeroom.

3. Add a safety factor to this amount to cover any unexpected sharp increases in business or to cover the possibility of a stock-out from the supplier.

4. Add the estimated amount of product used and the safety factor together to get the par stock of that item.

5. Place a label with the amount of the par stock on that item's shelf in the storeroom.

The amount delivered by a supplier brings an item back up to the par stock inventory level. In the standing order method, the supplier's delivery person comes in, takes inventory, and delivers the amount necessary to bring the item back up to its par stock level. The delivery person also removes any outdated stock and issues a credit to the restaurant or foodservice operation. While the standing order is a good purchasing method in theory, it is often abused. For example, an unscrupulous delivery person could bring in some fresh stock, take out some old stock, and shuffle the stock on the shelf. The delivery person gives the manager an invoice for the entire quantity on the shelf and says, "Sign here. I've rotated your stock and this is what I've left you." The manager signs the invoice and the delivery person leaves. What happened in this scenario is that fresh product was put in with some of the old product that was not removed, and the restaurant was charged for the entire quantity on the shelf, including the product it already owned. As a result, food cost increases, profit decreases, and the delivery person has product to sell for cash at a later stop. For the standing order method to be successful, the manager needs to ensure that the delivery person shows the manager the items being removed and those being brought in.

- **One-stop shop**—This method is becoming the most popular in purchasing goods today. It involves purchasing most, if not all, of an operation's goods from one supplier. Independent operators and chains both use this method. It came about when foodservice suppliers began merging with meatpackers, produce houses, bakeries, and dairies to form giant super-suppliers. In theory, it works well. Delivery costs are reduced with one truck stopping instead of several. Purchasing can be done online with the operation's specifications and par stocks loaded into the program. The downside is that if the supplier is out of an item, the operation is in trouble since there is no backup purveyor for that item. Also, since the buyer relies on the supplier's pricing rather than getting price quotes for items, the pricing might not be the most competitive for the restaurant or foodservice organization. The name "one-stop shop" is a misnomer, as most organizations that use this method do not purchase 100 percent of their goods from one-stop suppliers. For example, most restaurant or foodservice organizations probably buy 80 to 90 percent of their items from one-stop suppliers and purchase dairy, bakery, or produce items from another source.

- **Cost-plus**—This method is used primarily by chain operations, as independents do not have enough volume for the supplier to offer it to them. In this method, the chain purchases 100 percent of a particular product line—meat, for example—from one purveyor. That purveyor sells the product at the purveyor's invoice price plus an agreed-upon percentage for handling, delivery, and the purveyor's profit. Although this system could be used in conjunction with one-stop shop, it most often is used with several sources; i.e., one source for meat, one for produce, one for dairy, one for groceries, and so on. Chains that use the cost-plus method of purchasing are normally paying the lowest possible price for their goods even though the purveyors do not bid against each other.

- **Sealed bids**—Large foodservice units such as schools, colleges, hospitals, institutions, and government agencies primarily use sealed bids. In this method, foodservice operations calculate the amount of a product—dairy, for example—that they will need over a period of time, normally a year, and have suppliers bid on that amount. Usually, the lowest bidder is selected as the supplier for that product. The supplier delivers the entire order amount at one time or spreads out the deliveries over a specific time period.

- **Commissary**—This method is used almost exclusively by chains and franchised units. Quite often 100 percent of that operation's supplies will come from the commissary. In the commissary method, orders from individual units are consolidated. The commissary then purchases the consolidated quantity from the preferred suppliers. Normally these products include refrigerated, frozen, or packaged premade items that are produced to the company's standards. Any paper supplies printed with the company's logo will also come from the commissary. Frequently, the commissary is owned by the parent company of the chain or franchise.

It is important to remember that no matter what method or methods of purchasing are used, controls and safeguards, such as item specifications, purchase orders, price comparison, and sound receiving practices, must be implemented to ensure that order, receipt, and invoice discrepancies are either minimized or avoided altogether.

What to Pay: AP Price vs. EP Cost

Many buyers in the restaurant and foodservice industry select a purchasing method based on price alone. While it is human nature to want to buy goods at the lowest possible price, it is a good idea only if the product purchased matches the product specification. For example, assume you are purchasing ground beef for a standardized recipe requiring 80/20 (80 percent lean, 20 percent fat) ground beef. Buying ground beef at the lowest price could result in purchasing 70/30 ground beef. While the price would be low, the quality and yield would not meet the specification. Consequently, there might be no savings or possibly even a loss. If you specified 80/20 ground beef and all suppliers bid on 80/20 ground beef as well as the rest of your specification, then the lowest price would be the best value. It is important that you distinguish between the costs on a per serving basis and the costs as purchased, because product waste is not accounted for in the as purchased (AP) price and can increase the per serving cost.

Another way of selecting a purchasing method is to look for the best edible portion (EP) cost. Suppliers quote AP prices and paying this price might be fine for some items. However, since most products have less than 100 percent yield, calculating the EP cost will enable you to more accurately determine which supplier's price is best for your needs.

Think About It...

Given the various methods of purchasing products, which application would fit best with restaurant or foodservice organizations you are familiar with? Is a combination of methods always the best strategy?

Think About It...

How do "price" and "value" differ? Under what circumstances might value have more importance than price for a restaurant or foodservice organization?

There are two steps in calculating EP cost. The first step is to calculate the product's yield percentage. The **yield percentage** is the EP weight divided by the AP weight. To determine the product's yield percentage, two methods can be used. A **yield chart** is a register that gives the EP weight of products as opposed to the AP weight. (See *Exhibit 5g.*) These charts give an average yield percentage for most food products in use. Yield charts are available from the Food and Drug Administration (FDA) at *www.fda.gov*. They are also available in many professional cookbooks.

Exhibit 5g

Yield Chart for Chicken

Poultry as purchased	Unit of purchase	Yield as served	Description of portion as served	Size of portion (in ounces)		Portions per purchase unit
				As served	Edible portion[1]	
Ready-to-cook						
Broilers	1½ lb	70%	½ bird	8.3	5.4	2.00
Fryers	lb[2]	43%	Boned	3.0	3.0	2.29
Parts (from 2½-lb bird)						
Breast half	lb	67%	With bone	3.2	2.6	3.35
Drumstick	lb	72%	With bone	2.1	1.4	5.49
Thigh	lb	68%	With bone	2.2	1.6	4.95
Drumstick and thigh	lb	70%	With bone	4.3	3.1	2.60
Wing	lb	64%	With bone	1.6	0.8	6.40

[1]Includes edible skin [2]Based on 2½-lb bird as purchased; neck and giblets not served

The second method is to conduct a yield test. A **yield test** is an analysis done in an operation to determine the difference between a product's AP weight and its EP weight. Although it is time-consuming, this method is recommended because it is the most accurate. It is particularly important to use the yield test for products that constitute a major portion of the operation's purchasing dollar. To calculate a yield percentage, weigh the product when it arrives. The result is the AP weight. The first job is to clean, trim, and put the product into the form called for in the recipe (i.e., slice, dice, cut) and then weigh the product again. The result is the EP weight. Divide the EP weight by the AP weight to get the edible portion percentage (EP percent), or product yield percentage.

$$\text{EP weight} \div \text{AP weight} = \text{EP \%}$$

The second step in calculating EP cost is to divide the AP price by the product yield percentage.

AP price ÷ EP % = EP cost

For example, a case of iceberg lettuce weighs 30 pounds and costs $25.50. The lettuce is washed, its outer leaves and core are removed, and it is shredded as called for in the recipe. The lettuce is weighed again. The weight now is 24 pounds. The EP cost for 30 pounds of usable lettuce is:

24 ÷ 30 = 0.80 or 80%

$25.50 ÷ 0.80 = $31.88

The cost per pound of the lettuce is $0.85 AP ($25.50/30) or $1.06 EP ($31.88/30). The cost per ounce is $0.05 AP ($0.85/16) or $0.07 EP ($1.06/16).

The buyer should be more concerned with the EP cost and must always ask the question, "What is the true cost of this product?" By using the yield test and calculating the EP cost, you can determine the real cost of a product to your operation.

Activity

Calculating EP Percentage and EP Cost

For each item, calculate the EP %, EP cost per pound, and EP cost per ounce.

	Item A	Item B	Item C
AP weight	60 lb	40 lb	80 lb
EP weight	55 lb	35 lb	70 lb
AP price per pound	$2.75	$2.25	$8.50
EP %			
EP cost per pound			
EP cost per ounce			

Other Factors That Influence Purchasing

In addition to the factors mentioned above, there are several other factors that can influence the price a supplier quotes. Complacency is one of these factors. The purchasing methods listed above, with the exception of competitive quotes and sealed bids, all allow for management to become content with whom they are doing business. Periodically, other suppliers should be called in to bid on the business. By doing this, management might find out that they could save money by changing suppliers or confirm that the company they are presently doing business with is indeed charging them the lowest possible price.

An additional factor influencing the price a supplier quotes to a buyer is how promptly the restaurant is paying its invoices. If an operation pays cash, the supplier often offers a discount of 2 to 3 percent. On the other hand, if an operation is habitually late in paying its bills, the supplier will charge a higher price for the items ordered. This is done to cover the supplier's costs in "carrying" the restaurant or foodservice operation. Remember, the supplier is also running a business and must pay for its inventory. A slow-paying customer will slow the supplier's cash flow and force the supplier to borrow money to pay for its inventory. Borrowing money increases the supplier's cost of doing business. This increased cost is passed on to the slow-paying customer.

The last factor that can influence price has to do with the acceptance of supplier gifts and rewards. Accepting gifts is a major ethical dilemma facing the industry today. Suppliers use various methods to influence a buyer's purchasing decisions. One method some suppliers use is to give gifts and rewards to buyers who purchase from them or who are planning to purchase from them. If a supplier recognizes that a buyer will accept gifts, the supplier will often continue giving gifts. They could be tickets to a ball game, free cases of wine, steaks, or other goods or services. Eventually, the buyer begins to feel obligated to purchase solely from that purveyor and ends up paying a higher price because the purveyor covers the cost

Activity

What Would You Do?

You are the general manager of a sports bar in Boston. A representative of your beer supplier has offered you four box seat tickets to a Red Sox game. You accept.

Later that fall, the same representative offers to fly you and a friend to Chicago for the weekend. The trip includes accommodations at a five-star hotel, meals at first-class restaurants, and tickets to the World Series to see the Cubs play the White Sox. You accept.

Break up into small groups and discuss the following questions:

1. Is the first situation ethical on your part?

2. Is the second situation ethical on your part?

3. If you decide that the first one is ethical and the second one is not, where do you draw the line?

4. Is it ethical of the representative to offer either gift?

5. How might this affect your cost of doing business with this firm?

of its gifts in the prices charged to its customers. Some restaurant and foodservice operations have a policy of accepting no gifts, while others place a low dollar limit, such as $25, on the value of gifts that the operation can accept. If there is no company policy, the buyer must decide where to draw the line. The more prudent buyer will accept no gifts.

When to Purchase

One of the controls in purchasing is when, or how often, to purchase. Consider that the very act of purchasing costs money, not only in product cost, but in organizational cost as well. It takes time to receive bids, complete purchase orders, phone in or electronically transmit orders, receive the goods, store the goods, and pay the invoices. Not to mention that the more often a purveyor's truck stops, the more the costs to the purveyor (and consequently the restaurant or foodservice organization) go up as well.

It would stand to reason, then, that less frequent orders would be best for the organization. However, this is not always true for two reasons. First, with fewer orders being placed, the inventory level must be higher. High levels of inventory tie up the organization's cash flow. Cash is not only tied up in the cost of the food but also in the cost of the storage space. Storage space, while necessary, does not generate sales but is a cost to the operation. Storage space costs money to build and may take space away from other functional areas such as dining space. In addition to the cost to build storage space, there is a cost to maintaining it. Pest control and regular cleaning are two of the costs of maintenance. In addition, some storage, such as cold storage, requires cooling and ventilation equipment that runs on electricity, thereby increasing utility costs. All of these costs associated with storage space must be covered by the sales brought in by the operation. Second, not all of the goods purchased lend themselves to being stored for any length of time. To optimize the timing of purchases, goods are broken down into two categories:

Exhibit 5h

Examples of perishable goods

Examples of nonperishable goods

- **Perishable goods** are products that have a relatively short shelf life—usually one to three days. Some perishable goods might last a few days longer, but their quality and yield would be considerably diminished. *Exhibit 5h* illustrates some of the items that are classified as perishable.

- **Nonperishable goods** are products that have a relatively longer shelf life. Nonperishable goods can last for a few months to a year if stored and handled properly. *Exhibit 5h* illustrates some of the items that are classified as nonperishable.

Perishable goods should be purchased as often as possible. In larger restaurant or foodservice operations, perishable goods could be purchased daily. In smaller operations, purchasing perishable goods every two to three days is considered reasonable. However, even smaller operations should not put off purchasing perishable goods longer than three days.

Nonperishable goods, on the other hand, should be purchased as seldom as possible for reasons previously given. The size of the storage area, the operation's cash flow, and location—urban versus rural—are all factors that the buyer must consider when determining how often to order nonperishable goods. Some operations purchase nonperishable food weekly, some bimonthly, and others monthly.

Perishable Quantity to Purchase

As mentioned earlier, perishables should be purchased as often as needed. To keep the product as fresh as possible, only the amount that is needed should be purchased. Therefore, it is necessary to take inventory each time perishables are ordered. To facilitate this process, a bid sheet should be used. A bid sheet is a listing of items needed and is used to get price quotes from suppliers. These are the steps that you should perform in determining the amount to purchase:

1. Determine the amount of product needed until the next delivery.

2. Inventory what is on hand.

3. Subtract what is on hand from the amount needed.

4. The result of this calculation is the amount to purchase.

By following this method, the operation is assured of having only the freshest product available for service to the customer.

Another method of purchasing specific types of perishables is the standing order. As mentioned earlier in this chapter, the delivery person leaves merchandise that brings the item's inventory back up to a predetermined level. This method is quite satisfactory as long as the supplier removes the unused stock and gives proper credit. If proper stock rotation does not occur, the operation is using product that is not as fresh as it should be, which could result in dissatisfied customers. The standing order method has the advantage of saving management time, but should be used only if the supplier agrees to give credit for excess inventory.

Exhibit 5i

Taking inventory on a regular basis ensures that stock is kept at the par stock level.

Nonperishable Quantity to Purchase: The Par Stock Method

Today in the restaurant and foodservice industry, the most common method used for determining the quantity of nonperishables to purchase is the par stock method. This method works well in operations that have a relatively steady flow of business and a menu that does not change frequently. The key to this method is assigning to every item in the storeroom a level that should be constantly on hand. When it is time to order, inventory the item and subtract that number from the par stock number. The resulting number is the amount to order. (See *Exhibit 5i.*)

For example, a restaurant famous for its fried chicken serves green beans seasoned with smoked ham chunks and onion as one of its side dishes. It uses one case of canned green beans each day, except on Saturday and Sunday when it uses two cases a day. Therefore, its usage is nine cases a week. Management has decided to add a safety factor of three cases. Consequently, its par stock for green beans is twelve cases. The restaurant receives a grocery delivery weekly. When the manager orders, he or she subtracts inventory from par stock for each item that needs to be ordered. When taking inventory of the green beans, the manager finds four cases on the shelf. The manager subtracts four (stock on hand) from twelve (par stock) and orders eight cases of green beans.

In larger operations, such as a hotel food and beverage department, requisitions are used to retrieve items from the storeroom. In this case, the storeroom manager has a spreadsheet for every item in the storeroom and subtracts the requisitioned amount from the inventory on the spreadsheet. When placing an order, the manager looks on the spreadsheet to determine the quantity currently on hand. This is known as a theoretical, or perpetual, inventory and is used rather than taking a physical inventory. Details of this procedure will be covered in the next chapter.

There are also software programs available that use the theoretical inventory approach to the par stock method of ordering. These programs can be used for large and small operations alike. Some of the more sophisticated programs are tied into the point-of-sale (POS) system in the restaurant or foodservice operation. In these programs, when a customer orders an item from the menu, all the food used in preparing that menu item is immediately taken out of inventory. When the inventory is depleted to a predetermined level, the program subtracts the amount on hand from the par stock quantity and generates a purchase order for that item. For example, if a customer orders a hamburger, when the server enters the order into the POS system, the program subtracts one hamburger bun, four ounces of ground beef, three pickle slices, one-quarter ounce of ketchup, and so on from inventory. As more hamburgers are ordered, more of these ingredients are subtracted from inventory. When the inventory for ground beef reaches a predetermined level of fifty pounds, the program subtracts fifty pounds from the par stock of 150 pounds, and notifies management to purchase one hundred pounds of ground beef.

Activity

Calculating Par Stock Amount to Order

1. A restaurant uses 1.5 gallons of Italian dressing a day and is open 7 days a week. Management wishes to have a safety factor of 4 gallons. The dressing comes packed 4 gallons to the case and the supplier will not break cases. Deliveries are weekly.

   What is the par stock, in gallons, of this item?_____

   How many cases should be ordered if there are 5 gallons on hand?_____

2. One fast-food establishment uses 1,248 buns a day and is open 7 days a week. The buns come in bags of 24 and are in boxes of 4 bags. The supplier will not sell partial boxes. Management wishes to have a safety factor of 96 buns or 4 bags. Delivery is weekly.

   What is the par stock, in boxes, of this item?_____

   How many boxes should be ordered if there are 55 boxes on hand?_____

AP Amount versus EP Amount

AP amount and EP amount also come into play when determining how much to purchase. To determine the AP amount to purchase, divide the EP amount needed by the yield percentage.

EP amount needed ÷ Yield percentage = AP amount

For example, the chef tells the buyer that she needs fifty pounds of cauliflower ready to use. The buyer looks up the yield of cauliflower and finds that its yield percent is 55 percent. The buyer purchases ninety-one pounds of cauliflower.

50 pounds needed ÷ 55% or .55 = 90.9 pounds

Some in the industry use the as served, or AS, amount because they say that EP is the amount before cooking. Most products will lose volume when cooked. Taking cooking loss into consideration, EP becomes **as served (AS)**, which is the amount available to serve to the customer. Others in the industry say that EP includes cooking loss and that is why they use this term. In this guide, EP is used and it includes cooking loss.

Activity

Calculating the Amount to Purchase Using EP and Yield Percent

1 An item that weighs 1 pound AP yields 12 ounces. You need 25 pounds EP. How many pounds AP should you purchase? _____

2 An item that weighs 3 pounds AP yields 2.25 pounds. You need 40 pounds EP. How many pounds AP should you purchase? _____

3 An item that weighs 12 ounces AP yields 8 ounces. You need 15 pounds EP. How many pounds AP should you purchase? _____

Catering Purchases

While the par stock method of calculating order quantities works for most operations, it will not work for all. Restaurant and foodservice operations that cater one-time special events, such as banquets, need to purchase items specifically for that occasion. Additionally, the amount purchased must be accurate since the caterer does not want to run out or have too much leftover. To calculate how much product to purchase, the caterer must know the menu, portion size, number of guests, and the product yield. The caterer follows the steps below to calculate the purchasing quantity:

1 Determine the number of servings per purchasing unit (SPU) by dividing the purchasing unit by the portion size. The purchasing unit and the portion size must be in the same unit of measure. For example, if the portion size is in ounces, the purchasing unit must be in ounces.

Purchasing unit ÷ Portion size = Servings per purchasing unit (SPU)

2 Determine the purchase factor (PF) by multiplying the SPU by the edible portion yield percent (EP %).

SPU × EP % = Purchase factor (PF)

3 Determine the amount to purchase by dividing the number of guests by the purchasing factor (PF).

Number of guests ÷ PF = Amount to purchase

For example, a catering company is going to serve 350 guests a 6-ounce portion of roast round of beef. The yield on a top round is 75 percent, including cooking loss. The purchasing unit is 16 ounces.

Think About It...

Why is order accuracy so important to a restaurant or foodservice organization that caters a special event? What might a caterer do with the food leftover from a special event?

16 oz ÷ 6 oz = 2.67

2.67 × .75 = 2.00

350 ÷ 2.00 = 175 pounds of top round to purchase

If the caterer also were to serve three ounces of fresh sugar snap peas with a yield of 95 percent, the amount to purchase would be calculated as follows:

16 oz ÷ 3 oz = 5.33

5.33 × .95 = 5.06

350 ÷ 5.06 = 69.17 (round to 70) pounds of sugar snap peas to purchase

Activity

Calculating the Amount to Purchase in Catering Services

1. You are serving a 4-ounce portion of an item to 750 guests. The item has an edible portion yield of 55 percent. How many pounds should you purchase?

2. You are serving a 10-ounce portion of an item to 180 salespeople. The item has an edible portion yield of 80 percent. How many pounds should you purchase?

3. You are serving an 8-ounce portion of an item to 275 guests. The item has an edible portion yield of 85 percent. How many pounds should you purchase?

Butcher Test

With the advent of boxed meats and portion-controlled cuts, the butcher test, also known as the meat yield test, is not used as often in the foodservice industry as it used to be. To ensure that they are making the most cost-conscious purchasing decision, some meat buyers for larger operations, such as major hotels, institutions, or colleges, still conduct a butcher test to determine the EP cost for a cut of meat.

The **butcher test** is a process in which a wholesale cut of meat is broken down into a retail cut and the trim, bone, and waste are analyzed and recorded to arrive at an EP cost for the retail cut. As a result of this process, the price per pound of the wholesale cut changes dramatically. When breaking down a wholesale cut, there is some loss. Depending on the cut, the loss could be considerable, while sometimes it is small. Some of the loss is usable, such as bones and trimmings for the stockpot, small cuts for stew or soups, or scraps for grinding. This loss can have value to the operation. Some of the other loss is not usable and therefore has no value.

The following example of a butcher test on beef tenderloin illustrates how the cost is determined. The top section of the form seen in *Exhibit 5j* contains general information. The name and the AP weight of the item are listed. The primary use of the item, in this case steaks, is listed next. The portion size of the steaks, the AP cost per pound, and the total cost are also listed, and the supplier and the date the test was conducted are noted.

Exhibit 5j

Butcher Test for Beef Tenderloin

Item	Beef Tenderloin		Weight	lb 8 oz 0
Used for	Steaks		Portion	8 oz
Price AP	$10.00 Per Pound		Total price	$80.00
Supplier	Bridgeport Meat Packing Co.		Date	02/20/06

Trim Breakdown	Weight	Market Value	Total Value
Fat/silver skin	1 lb 6 oz	0	0
Tenderloin strips	1 lb 12 oz	$7.00	$12.25
Ground beef	6 oz	$1.75	$ 0.66
Total	3 lb 8 oz	Total	$12.91

Weight AP	8 lb 0 oz	Total price AP	$80.00
Less: trim weight	3 lb 8 oz	Trim total	$12.91
Yield of item	4 lb 8 oz	Net price	$67.09

Net price ÷ Yield of item = Cost per pound EP

$67.09 ÷ 4 lb 8 oz or 4.5 lb = $14.91

After the wholesale cut is broken down and cut into steaks, the leftover elements are recorded in the next section of the form. In this case, the silver skin was trimmed off and the fat cover removed. These parts have no value and were recorded as such. The ends of the tenderloin were cut into tips with a retail value of $7.00 per pound. The retail value is determined by contacting a supplier to get the current price of the item. The weight multiplied by the market value is listed under total value. Some scraps that were too small to be cut into tips were ground into ground beef at a retail value of $1.75 per pound. The weight of the trim is totaled and the dollar value of the trim is totaled. After these are determined, the results can be used to calculate the EP cost per pound as follows:

The weight of the trim is subtracted from the AP weight of the tenderloin to determine the yield weight.

8 pounds − 3.5 pounds = 4.5 pounds yield weight

The total value of the trim is subtracted from the total AP price to determine the net price of the tenderloin.

$80.00 − $12.91 = $67.09 net price

The net price is divided by the yield of the tenderloin to determine the EP cost per pound.

$67.09 ÷ 4.5 = $14.91 EP cost per pound

As you compare the AP price per pound and the EP cost per pound, you can see that there is a sizable difference between the AP price of $10.00 per pound and the EP cost of $14.91 per pound. It is understandable why buyers are more concerned about EP cost than AP price. Now the buyer can compare the EP cost of the trim cuts from the wholesale cut with the EP cost of ready-made portion control cuts to determine the most cost-effective way to purchase this item in the future.

Activity

Butcher Test for Turkey

Complete the following butcher test problem. Fill in the blanks that will complete the test.

Item	Turkey breast		Weight	lb 5 oz 0
Used for	Turkey sandwiches		Portion	3 oz
Cost AP	$1.45 **Per** Pound		Total cost	
Supplier	Chick's Chickens		Date	06/12/06

Trim Breakdown	Weight	Market Value	Total Value
Fat, skin	8 oz	$0.04	$0.02
Bone	1 lb 10 oz	$0.05	$0.08
Total	2 lb 2 oz	Total	$0.10

Weight AP _____   Total cost AP _____

Less: trim weight _____   Trim total _____

Yield of item _____   Net cost _____

Net cost ÷ Yield of item = Cost per pound EP   _____

Receiving Procedures and Cost Control

Once you have examined the purchasing costs, another area to review is the receiving procedure. It is one of the simplest controls in the restaurant and foodservice industry, yet many managers take an apathetic approach to it. This is unfortunate since the potential for loss in this area is extremely high. Consider this typical scenario:

It is midmorning in the busy kitchen of a large restaurant. A delivery truck arrives. The driver unloads the order and puts it in the receiving area of the kitchen, and looks for the chef. He finds the chef adding ingredients to the steam kettle in the back of the kitchen and stirring the contents. The driver says, "I've got your order in the back of the kitchen, here's the invoice." The chef says, "I'm busy—hey, Joe, sign this guy's invoice. I don't have time to deal with this now." Joe signs the invoice and the driver leaves.

The order sits in the back of the kitchen until after the noon rush. The meat and produce have been at room temperature for four hours. The frozen goods are partially thawed. The chef tells Joe to put the order up. Nobody knows that part of the order is missing.

Unfortunately, this scenario is more common than not. Without anyone realizing it, the food cost in this operation has just increased and the quality of ingredients that the staff has to work with has diminished. To avoid this situation, managers should follow these receiving procedures (see *Exhibit 5k*):

1. **Have the delivery person put the order in the receiving area of the kitchen.**

2. **Obtain a copy of the purchase order.**

3. **Also have a copy of the purchasing specifications available.**

4. **Check the delivery quantity against both the invoice and the purchase order.** This will tell you if any unauthorized items were added to the order. If the items are purchased by count, count them. If purchased by weight, weigh them, particularly meat and produce. Also, check the delivery quality against the organization's purchasing specifications. Open the boxes. Look at the produce. Is it fresh, the right color, the correct size, the precise

Exhibit 5k

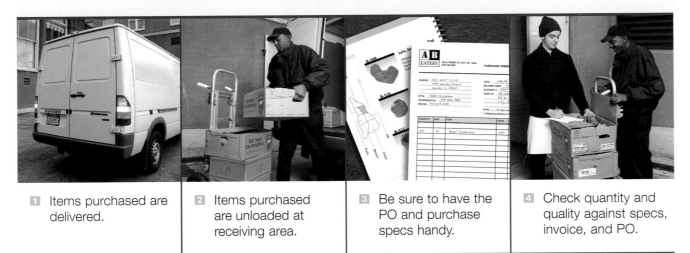

Receiving Procedures and Controls

1. Items purchased are delivered.

2. Items purchased are unloaded at receiving area.

3. Be sure to have the PO and purchase specs handy.

4. Check quantity and quality against specs, invoice, and PO.

Think About It...

Have you ever observed what happens in your place of employment regarding the receiving process? What happens at work isn't always the best way. How might you improve the process that you observed?

degree of ripeness, and not bruised or rusted? Is the meat fresh, the flesh and fat the right color, USDA stamped? Is the fish fresh, clear eyes, tight scales, and firm to the touch? Is the fresh poultry properly iced? Check the temperature of all meat, fresh poultry, fish, dairy, and frozen goods.

5 **Compare the prices on the invoice to those on the purchase order to ensure that they match.** Check the math on the invoice, even if it is a computer-generated invoice.

6 **If everything is in order, sign the invoice.** If something must be returned, have the driver write out a credit memo for the item or circle the item on the invoice and state the reason for the return. Use the same procedure if an item is missing. The driver may wish to rush you through this procedure. Do not be swayed! The objective here is to make sure you have the correct product, quality, and quantity at the correct price. If any of these elements are missing, the food cost will likely increase and the profit will subsequently decrease.

7 **Put the goods away promptly.** Dairy, meat, fresh poultry, and fresh fish first, then frozen food, produce, and dry goods. This order is very important to protect against product deterioration and possible theft. When the goods have been put up, secure the storage area.

8 **Process the paperwork by sending copies of the signed purchase order and the signed invoice to the accounting department.**

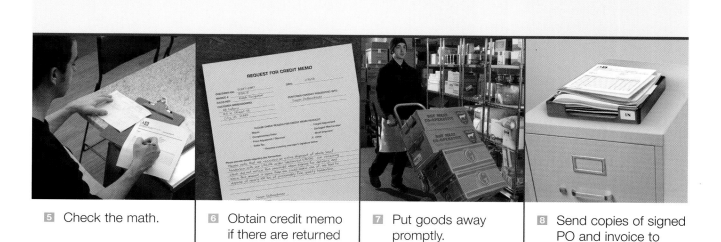

| 5 Check the math. | 6 Obtain credit memo if there are returned or missing items. | 7 Put goods away promptly. | 8 Send copies of signed PO and invoice to accounting. |

The receiving control process is not difficult to follow and, if done consistently, can ensure that costs are in line with the restaurant or foodservice operation's specifications. In addition, three separate individuals should execute the procedures of purchasing, receiving, and paying the bills to prevent theft and embezzlement. In a small operation, assigning separate individuals for purchasing, receiving, and bill paying should be followed to the extent possible. It is vital for the manager to understand that receiving is very important to the overall control system of an operation and to ensure that receiving procedures are followed.

Summary

Purchasing and receiving are other dimensions in the development of controls in restaurant or foodservice operations. While they are important elements, they are often overlooked in day-to-day operations. Two critical controls are the purchase order and the specification, which tie together the purchasing, receiving, and accounting functions. Other controls include purchasing the correct amount and knowing exactly what is being paid for each item. Calculating AP and EP, as well as conducting butcher tests, gives the buyer the critical information needed to make prudent purchases. Knowing when to purchase is also part of a sound purchasing strategy. Perishables, which need to be turned over quickly, must be purchased more often than nonperishable goods. However, even the level of nonperishable goods needs to be sufficient to conduct business, but not so high as to negatively impact cash flow.

The proper receiving procedure includes checking goods against the purchase order and invoice for count, weight, and price. The quality of the goods should also be compared to the product specifications to ensure that they meet the operation's standards. Finally, the last step in the process is to put goods away promptly to avoid shrinkage, spoilage, and theft.

Review Your Learning

1 Proper purchasing involves

  A. purchasing the highest quality available.

  B. purchasing according to the specification at the lowest price.

  C. purchasing at the lowest price.

  D. Both A and B

2 A primary control in the purchasing process is

  A. the purchase order.

  B. the specification.

  C. the USDA grading system.

  D. Both A and B

3 A purchase order is circulated to

  A. the supplier.

  B. the accounting department.

  C. the receiving clerk.

  D. A, B, and C

4 Specifications are circulated to

  A. the supplier.

  B. the accounting department.

  C. the receiving clerk.

  D. A, B, and C

5 If an item costs $3.50 per pound AP and its weight is 10 pounds AP and 7 pounds EP, the total EP cost of that item is

  A. $50.00.

  B. $35.00.

  C. $24.50.

  D. $14.29.

6 Using the data from the previous problem, if 30 pounds EP of the item were needed, the pounds purchased AP would be

  A. 30.

  B. 43.

  C. 20.

  D. 21.

7 Perishable goods should be ordered

  A. daily.

  B. every two to three days.

  C. Either A or B

  D. Neither A nor B

8 Examples of nonperishable goods are

  A. canned goods.

  B. dry goods.

  C. frozen goods.

  D. A and B only

9 You are purchasing an item for a banquet for 400 persons, the portion of that item is 4 ounces, it costs $2.85 per pound, and its yield is 85 percent. How many pounds should you purchase?

  A. 118

  B. 188

  C. 340

  D. 200

10 When receiving goods, the goods should be checked against the

  A. invoice.

  B. purchase order.

  C. specification.

  D. A, B, and C

continued on next page

Review Your Learning *continued from previous page*

11 **A purchase order is**

  A. a form used to list the goods ordered, their price, and delivery date, plus other relevant data.

  B. circulated from the buyer to the supplier, receiving clerk, and accounting department.

  C. Both A and B

  D. Neither A nor B

12 **Which of the following method(s) would a small, independent restaurateur probably use in purchasing canned and dry goods?**

  A. Sealed bids

  B. Competitive quotes

  C. A commissary

  D. Standing order

13 **In which method(s) of purchasing would a specification be used?**

  A. Competitive quote

  B. One-stop shop

  C. Sealed bid

  D. All of the above

14 **Which of the following is the most correct statement regarding the purchasing of perishable and nonperishable goods?**

  A. Perishables should be ordered every one, two, or three days.

  B. Perishables and nonperishables should be ordered weekly.

  C. Nonperishables should be ordered every one, two, or three days.

  D. If ordered from a commissary, both perishables and nonperishables are ordered monthly.

15 **Par stock is**

  A. an item that a restaurant has on hand at all times.

  B. the level that must be continually in stock from one delivery to another.

  C. a method of purchasing by which each item in the storeroom has a level at which it is reordered.

  D. the amount of an item ordered each week.

16 **You have determined that the chef uses one case of tomato sauce per day and that the safety stock should be three cases. You order tomato sauce once a week. Your inventory shows that there are three cases left. The chef will use one case before the order arrives. How many cases should you order?**

  A. 3

  B. 5

  C. 7

  D. 8

Controlling Food Costs in Storage and Issuing

6

Inside This Chapter

- ■ Using Proper Storage Techniques to Control Food Costs
- ■ Inventory Control
- ■ Perpetual versus Physical Inventory

After completing this chapter, you should be able to:

- ■ Describe food storage techniques used to control theft.
- ■ Explain the FIFO method of stock rotation.
- ■ Describe the proper method of taking inventory.
- ■ Describe the various methods of inventory pricing.
- ■ Calculate inventory turnover rate and inventory value.
- ■ Compare physical inventory to perpetual inventory, or theoretical inventory.
- ■ Calculate a daily food cost.

Test Your Knowledge

1. **True or False:** The amount of time and the temperature at which canned and dry goods are stored is irrelevant. *(See p. 90.)*

2. **True or False:** FIFO is an inventory pricing system. *(See p. 89.)*

3. **True or False:** LIFO is a stock system that uses the oldest product first. *(See p. 90.)*

4. **True or False:** The actual act of taking an inventory should be done by two people. *(See p. 96.)*

5. **True or False:** Daily food cost is an estimated food cost. *(See p. 106.)*

6. **True or False:** The figure for opening inventory is the same as the figure for the closing inventory of the previous period. *(See p. 102.)*

7. **True or False:** A perpetual inventory should be compared to a physical inventory to see if there is any shrinkage or loss of product in the storeroom. *(See p. 95.)*

8. **True or False:** Establishing a par stock for each item in a workstation in the kitchen or bar will reduce the risk of running out of an item during a rush period. *(See p. 93.)*

9. **True or False:** Theft of goods while they are in storage is a major reason that an operation's food costs increase. *(See p. 92.)*

Key Terms

Actual price method

Averaged price method

Daily food cost

Extending

FIFO method

Inventory

Inventory breakdown

Inventory turnover

Issuing

Latest price method

LIFO method

Padding

Perpetual inventory

Physical inventory

Requisitions

Time and temperature control

Transfer

Introduction

While it is important to ensure that the restaurant or foodservice operation receives the correct food products at the correct price, the manager's responsibility for controlling food costs does not end there. An operation's manager wants to prevent additional food costs due to spoilage, theft, or out-of-control inventory. This chapter explores some of the ways a manager can properly control food storage and inventory, as well as how to price inventory and determine inventory turnover.

Using Proper Storage Techniques to Control Food Costs

As a manager, you need to realize that food products and the food inventory they represent are the equivalent of money to your operation. A filet mignon in the walk-in freezer represents a selling price point to the operation and an amount that can be revenue when sold to a customer. If for some reason that filet spoils or disappears from your walk-in freezer, the potential revenue is also lost. In addition, your operation has already incurred the cost of purchasing the filet. The savvy manager learns quickly that product integrity and security are critical components to a successful operation.

Given that product spoilage and lack of security can reduce the profits of an operation, it is critical to implement processes that minimize or eliminate the potential for these two factors to occur.

Controlling Spoilage

After theft, spoilage is the second biggest cause of loss in the storeroom. While theft is difficult to control, spoilage is fairly easy to manage. Consider that spoilage is most often caused by carelessness and by not following correct procedures to protect the integrity of the product. The three principle causes of spoilage are:

■ Improper stock rotation

■ Time and temperature abuse

■ Inadequate sanitation practices

Stock Rotation: FIFO

The restaurant and foodservice industry generally uses the first in, first out (FIFO) method of rotating stock. The **FIFO method** is commonly used to ensure that refrigerated, frozen, and dry products are properly rotated during storage. Using FIFO helps guarantee that the inventory is turned over in a proper manner. In the FIFO method, an older product is used prior to a more recently purchased product. The FIFO method as a way of using the latest price to value inventory will be discussed later in this chapter.

The key to the success of the FIFO method relies on two people: the receiving clerk and the person using the product. After the food has been properly received, the receiving clerk writes the date received on the package, and puts the goods on the shelf by placing the newest product at the back of the shelf and moving the oldest product forward. Some food products have "use by" or "sell by" dates assigned by the processor. These should be stocked by the processor's supplied date. The person using the product should take the oldest product at the front of the shelf. For processor-dated product, it is extremely important for the staff member using these products to check the date prior to using the product. For whatever reason, these two steps in using the FIFO method do not always happen. Sometimes, the receiving clerk decides that it is easier to simply put the goods on the shelf without rotating them, and quite often cooks will hunt for fresh ingredients rather than use something a little older.

Management needs to keep constant vigil in the storeroom, coolers, and freezers to ensure that proper rotation is being followed. If proper rotation does not occur, eventually the older items—perishables in particular—will have to be thrown out because their quality no longer meets company standards. When this happens, food cost increases and profit decreases.

Another method of stock rotation is the LIFO method. The **LIFO method**, which means "last in, first out," is a system of stock rotation in which the last item received is the first item used. This method is not used very often due to spoilage concerns.

Time and Temperature Control

The moment that fruit and vegetables are harvested, they begin deteriorating. As soon as meat and poultry are processed and fish and seafood are harvested from the water, they begin to decline. Some products deteriorate more quickly than others, and these products must be given special attention. During storage, some products, while perfectly good in taste and texture, will shrink. This shrinkage causes yield loss, which increases food cost. While there are methods that have been devised to slow the deterioration process, eventually all food products will deteriorate to the point at which they are no longer good for consumption. Because of product deterioration, time is not on the side of food products.

Proper purchasing (particularly of perishables), promptly putting stock up after receiving, and correct stock rotation all go a long way in slowing the deterioration process. However, perhaps nothing is more important in holding food as proper time and temperature control. **Time and temperature control** is having policies and procedures in place that monitor the amount of time and correct temperature of food products in the flow of food. Different food products have different temperature requirements. Dry goods benefit from storage at the proper temperature. *Exhibit 6a* identifies the recommended holding temperatures for a variety of food. The manager or staff member responsible for the storage area should check the temperature of the refrigerators, freezers, and other storage areas on a regular basis to be sure the temperatures are in the

Exhibit 6a

Food Holding Temperatures

Dry storage
50°F to 70°F (10°C to 21°C)

Fresh fruit and vegetables
Vary depending on product

Eggs and dairy
41°F (5°C) or below
Eggs at 45°F (7°C) or below

Meat and poultry
41°F (5°C) or below

Fish
41°F (5°C) or below

correct range. Keeping storage facilities in the proper temperature range helps to ensure the longest possible usable life of the food products within. It is important to monitor the internal temperature of food to ensure they are at the right temperature.

Sanitation Practices

High levels of sanitation should always be practiced in all areas of the restaurant or foodservice operation. The storage areas are no exception. In the storeroom, food should be stored away from the walls and 6″ off the floor to allow for sweeping and mopping, which should be done daily. Shelving should be made of durable metal, preferably stainless steel. Dry goods such as beans, rice, flour, and sugar should be stored in airtight containers. The walls and floor of the storeroom should be made of a nonporous material that is easy to clean. Insect and rodent control should be performed on a regular basis, preferably monthly, or more often if needed.

Walk-in and reach-in refrigerators and freezers should be wiped down on a daily basis and deep cleaned on a weekly basis. The shelves, walls, floors, and ceilings should be noncorrosive metal, preferably stainless steel. The shelves should be slatted to allow for air circulation.

Product should be distributed evenly and not crowded, which also allows for air to circulate freely. It is particularly important that the refrigerated storage areas be kept clean and sanitized and that proper food rotation is enforced. By doing this, you will prevent odors from forming that can be absorbed by other foods, thus rendering them useless and causing an increase in food cost. Keeping a clean, secure storage area with properly rotated contents at the correct temperature will result in minimal, safe storage of food and food loss.

Exhibit 6b

An organized storeroom aids personnel in quickly finding needed products.

Storeroom Organization

A well-organized storeroom, as seen in *Exhibit 6b*, is an asset to any restaurant or foodservice operation and can help with reducing spoilage and theft. Every item in storage should have a specific place and it should always be in that place The shelves should be labeled with the name of the item and its par stock amount. This not only facilitates taking inventory, but also saves labor by kitchen personnel because they know exactly where each item is and do not have to waste time searching. All products should be labeled with the name and use by or expiration dates.

Controlling Security and Theft

Theft is one of the greatest threats to food while it is in storage. Consequently, food must be securely kept. Deciding exactly how to oversee secure food storage is a dilemma that has perplexed management over the years. If the storeroom is wide open, allowing staff to come and go and remove product as they please, these conditions encourage rampant theft. (See *Exhibit 6c.*) On the other hand, if the storeroom is securely locked at all times, when cooks run out of an item or need an ingredient for a customer request, they will have to locate management to unlock the storeroom every time. Obviously, this extreme control can cause significant delays in preparing a customer's order and could also cause other orders on the line to back up. It is clear that neither of these choices is desirable. While the storeroom should be secure at all times, there are two other ways in which this dilemma can be solved.

Exhibit 6c

Easily concealed items are most susceptible to theft.

First, a par stock should be established for each area in the operation. Par stock, as a purchasing control, was discussed in Chapter 5; however, par stock can apply to food storage control as well. Recall that par stock is the average use of an item for a given period plus a safety factor. In the case of food storage control, the given period of time is a shift. To establish a par stock for each item that is needed for the shift, first determine the average use of the item plus a safety factor, in case sales for that item spike. Prior to the rush, the person responsible for an area should obtain all of the ingredients necessary for that shift and bring them up to their par stock level. This is done under the supervision of the person responsible for that particular area. For example, the head chef or lead cook would supervise the procurement of supplies for the line, while the bar manager or head bartender would obtain or supervise the fulfillment of bar supplies. This is the same theory covered in Chapter 5 for purchasing control, except that instead of buying from an outside source, the item is being "purchased" from the storeroom. (See *Exhibit 6d*.)

Second, rather than have the manager be the only person with a set of storeroom keys, trusted employees should have keys to the area for which they are responsible. For example, the bar manager or head bartender would have keys to the liquor storeroom but not the meat cooler, while the chef or lead cook would have the keys to the meat cooler but not the liquor storeroom. In this way, should a bartender or line cook need an item, the person with the keys is

Exhibit 6d

The method of controlling food storage using par stock levels is similar to that used in purchasing supplies from an outside source, except in this case, you are "purchasing" supplies from your own storeroom.

Think About It...

Does your establishment have video cameras or other control devices for security? Do they work? Are they a good idea? What about using trust as a control device? Which is more important to a business—trust or security?

already in the area and can retrieve the needed items quickly. The person who is responsible for supplying the materials used in the operation follows a process of **issuing,** or taking the food or beverage products from storage.

While it is important to keep the inventory secure, remember that certain items are more susceptible to theft than others. Fifty-pound sacks of flour or sugar, #10 cans of corn, or five-gallon boxes of cola syrup are probably not going to be stolen. They are large, bulky, of little value, and hard to conceal and remove from the operation. While they could be stolen, they probably will not be, and management's efforts need to concentrate on items that are more likely to be stolen. These items include those that are easy to conceal and/or those that are high in value, such as liquor, wine, steaks, and coffee packs. These items must be under lock and key at all times. Some restaurant and foodservice operations have these areas under video surveillance.

Using one of these methods or a combination of methods can decrease theft and food loss.

Inventory Control

Keeping the storerooms organized and labeled properly is not only important in spoilage and theft prevention but also in the inventory process. The restaurant or foodservice manager needs to know how much product is on hand to support the operation's menu offerings. In other words, the manager needs to know the operation's inventory. An **inventory** is an itemized list of goods and products, their on-hand quantity, and their dollar value. With a known inventory, a restaurant or foodservice manager can calculate the cost of food sold as well as the inventory turnover rate. The total value of the operation's inventory is important since it is part of the assets on the balance sheet.

It is essential for a manager to understand the principles of inventory control and to be able to conduct an inventory. Physical inventory and perpetual inventory are two principles of inventory control that are particularly important. A **physical inventory** is an actual physical count and valuation of all items on hand. It usually is taken at the end of an accounting period. On the other hand, a **perpetual inventory** is a theoretical count based on goods received and issued. Perpetual inventory tries to eliminate the need for frequent counting by adding to the inventory when goods are received and by subtracting from the inventory when requisitions or issues occur. In larger operations, kitchen personnel use **requisitions,** which are forms that contain the specifics about the item(s) needed, to request items from the

Exhibit 6e

Sample Storeroom Requisition

Storeroom Requisition

Date: _____ Charge to: _____ Department: _____

Requisition approved by: _____

Requisition filled by: _____

Item	Requested quantity	Issued amount	Unit cost	Total cost
TOTAL				

storeroom. (See *Exhibit 6e.*) A perpetual inventory can be compared to the actual inventory to determine how much inventory shrinkage has occurred in the storage area. Perpetual inventory is a popular method to keep track of liquor and wine.

Recording the Inventory

Inventory should be taken periodically, corresponding with the frequency of the income statement. In most operations this is monthly. Some quick-service operations and bars take inventory weekly. Still others, while a rare occurrence, do inventory quarterly or annually. Regardless of when you take inventory or whether you are recording a physical inventory or keeping a perpetual inventory, an important point to remember is to build uniformity into your process by weighing or counting items consistently, using a consistent inventory pricing method, and taking inventory at a consistent time of day.

When the manager sets up a restaurant or foodservice operation's inventory process, he or she will want to consider what inventory breakdown to use. An **inventory breakdown** is a method of categorizing the operation's food and supplies. In some restaurant or foodservice operations, inventory is taken of all goods in the kitchen without regard to breakdown. In other operations, inventories are broken down into food and supplies. This breakdown is particularly important if food and supplies are separated on the income statement. Some operations further break down food into meat, dairy, bakery, produce, frozen goods, canned, and dry goods. Establishments may use all of these categories, or some of them, or may even need to use different ones. The determining factor is what food items an operation wants to track. For example, a steakhouse may want to track meat cost and would therefore categorize and inventory meat items separately from all other products in the kitchen. A quick-service operation

Exhibit 6f

Sample Inventory Sheet

Inventory					
Category:				Counted by: _____	
			Date: _____	Recorded by: _____	
Item	Count	Unit	Price	Unit	Total
TOTAL					
				Page _____ of _____	

may want to track paper supplies and will inventory these separately from the other supplies. You will learn later that inventory is instrumental in figuring the cost of goods sold.

When taking inventory, use two people. One person counts or weighs the items and the other person records it on the inventory sheet. (See *Exhibit 6f.*) This makes the process move more quickly, and more important, it reduces the possibility of "padding" the inventory for the purpose of reducing the food cost.

Start in one place and progress through the establishment in a logical manner. For example, start in the storeroom in the upper left-hand corner. Move through the storeroom going down every shelf from left to right. When the storeroom is inventoried, move on to the walk-in refrigerator and inventory it in the same manner as the storeroom, then inventory the walk-in freezer. In the kitchen, start in the left-hand corner and progress through the kitchen. Do not forget to inventory food and supplies, such as coffee, condiments, paper napkins, placemats, and straws in the service areas and dining room.

Some operations count everything in the kitchen, while some may estimate the amount for a few items. An example of estimating the amount might be in the use of spices. If the spice inventory is fairly consistent from period to period, a price is applied to all spices and recorded as "spices, one lot." Another example is the steam table and/or the pick-up line, which would be recorded as "goods in transit."

When the physical inventory is complete, the counts are turned over to management. At this point, if the operation uses a perpetual inventory system, management will compare the physical inventory to the perpetual inventory. Because restaurant operations are dynamic in nature, the physical inventory and perpetual inventory will most likely not match completely. Management will request a recount of any areas with large discrepancies. Having an accurate physical inventory is a critical preparatory step to inventory pricing.

Exhibit 6g

Comparison Chart of Pricing Methods

FIFO

The latest price paid for the item is recorded.

LIFO

The oldest price paid for the item is used.

Averaged Price

A composite of all prices paid is averaged and used.

Actual Price

The actual price is listed on the inventory for all items.

Inventory Pricing

Although recording an inventory will tell you what products are in stock and in what quantities, it will not tell you how much your operation's inventory is worth. Determining the worth of the inventory is an important next step because the dollar value of the inventory is reported on the operation's income statement. There are several methods of valuing items, as shown in *Exhibit 6g*. Whichever method is chosen, the manager will achieve the best results by using it consistently. Consistency in inventory pricing takes two forms. First, the price used for the item must be in the same unit as the count for the item. For example, if Kadota figs are counted by the can, then the pricing unit is per can. However, the invoice price for Kadota figs is per case. Therefore, the price per case must be converted to price per can. Second, the manager must use the chosen pricing method throughout every period. Not only is this important for providing reliable reports to management, but also for reporting income to the Internal Revenue Service.

The various pricing methods include:

- FIFO (first in, first out), also known as the **latest price method,** uses the latest price paid for a product to value an inventory. This method assumes that the oldest product is used first and that the most recent product, purchased at the most recent price, represents the majority of product on the shelf when inventory is taken. This is the most widely used pricing method in the restaurant and foodservice industry for two reasons. First, it is the easiest and quickest way to cost an inventory because management will use the latest invoices to research prices. Second, it tells management what the product in storage is worth in today's market. In this method, the latest price paid for the product is the one that is recorded in the price column on the inventory sheet. For example, if a case of green beans purchased at the start of the period cost $20.00 per case but a case bought towards the end of the period cost $21.00, when inventoried, both cases would be priced at $21.00.

- LIFO (last in, first out) is the opposite of the FIFO pricing method. The LIFO method is a method of inventory pricing in which the oldest price is the one used for valuing the inventory. This method assumes that the most recently purchased product is used first and that the product that is on the shelf, when inventoried, is the oldest. Therefore, the oldest price paid for that product is used to value the inventory. This method is not widely used in the foodservice industry because the typical practice is to use the oldest product first (FIFO) due to spoilage. In the green bean example given above, the product price would be recorded as $20.00 per case on the inventory sheet instead of the latest price of $21.00.

■ **Averaged price method** uses a composite of all prices paid for an item during the inventory period to valuate the inventory. The first step is to determine the cost of food available by adding purchases during the period to the opening inventory of the item. Then the averaged price is calculated by dividing the cost of food available for sale by the number of units available for sale. In the green bean example, assume that 5 cases were on hand at the beginning of the period at a cost of $19.00 per case (opening inventory), and that 5 cases were purchased at $20.00 per case and 5 cases at $21.00 per case. The averaged price would be $20.00 per unit. This is calculated as follows:

1 Calculate the cost of food available in inventory.

Opening inventory		
5 cases at $19.00		$ 95.00
Purchases		
5 cases at $20.00	$ 100.00	
5 cases at $21.00	$ 105.00	
	$ 205.00	$ 205.00
Cost of food available		$ 300.00

2 Calculate number of units available.

Number of units available for sale:

$$\textbf{Opening inventory } + \textbf{ Purchases } = \begin{array}{c}\textbf{Units available}\\\textbf{for sale}\end{array}$$

$$\textbf{5 cases } + \textbf{ 10 cases } = \textbf{ 15 cases}$$

3 Calculate inventory price per unit.

Inventory price per unit:

$$\frac{\textbf{Cost of food available}}{\textbf{Number of units available}} = \textbf{Inventory price per unit}$$

$$\frac{\textbf{\$300.00}}{\textbf{15 cases}} = \textbf{\$20.00}$$

It should be readily apparent that this method is not widely used in the foodservice industry. Because of the multiplicity of items in inventory, this method is too time-consuming to be practical. It is mentioned here solely because it is a recognized method of inventory valuation.

■ Actual price method is also known as the specific unit cost method. In the **actual price method,** the actual price paid for the product is the cost that is listed on the closing inventory sheet. Thus in the green bean example, there would be two lines—one line for the number of cases of green beans remaining at $20.00 per case, and another line for the number of cases in inventory at $21.00 per case. The actual price method takes discipline on the part of management. Every item that is received must be marked with its per unit cost. In the green bean example, the first cases received would be marked $20.00 since the inventory is by the case. If the green beans were inventoried by can, each can would have $3.33 written on it ($20.00 per case ÷ 6 #10 cans per case = $3.33). Every item in inventory must have its cost written on each unit for this method to be utilized. If the item is not marked, management will waste valuable time researching the cost of that item. The actual price method is the most accurate method of pricing inventory since the real cost of each item is reflected in the value of the closing inventory. Restaurant and foodservice organizations that use computerized inventory systems most often use the actual price method of inventory valuation.

Activity

Calculating Averaged Price

1 Opening inventory for frozen corn is 2 cases at $24.00 per case. During the period, 4 cases were purchased at $25.00 per case and 6 cases at $28.00 per case. What is the averaged price per case? _____

2 Opening inventory for peas is 5 cases at $18.00 per case. During the period, 3 cases were purchased at $21.00 per case and 4 cases at $22.00 per case. What is the averaged price per case? _____

3 Opening inventory for tomato paste is 3 cases at $11.00 per case. During the period, 5 cases were purchased at $14.00 per case. What is the averaged price per case? _____

Extending and Totaling

After the inventory has been counted, recorded, and priced, it is then extended and totaled. **Extending** the inventory means multiplying the number of units of each item by the item's unit price. For example, 8 cases of cherry pie filling priced at $34.00 per case would be $272.00.

Number of units × Unit price = Total cost of inventoried item

8 × $34.00 = $272.00

Exhibit 6h

Sample Dairy Inventory

Inventory

Category: Dairy

Date: 12-05

Counted by: G.B.

Recorded by: M.K.

Item	Count	Unit	Price	Unit	Total
Milk, Homogenized	2	5 gal	15.75	5 gal	$ 31.50
Milk, Homogenized	20	gal	3.25	gal	65.00
Milk, Homogenized	125	½ Pt	0.21	½ Pt	26.25
Milk, 2%	140	½ Pt	0.19	½ Pt	26.60
Cream, heavy	8	qt	6.75	qt	54.00
Cream, half & half	15	qt	4.15	qt	62.25
Cream, sour	20	qt	3.55	qt	71.00
Butter	79	lb	2.69	lb	212.51
Butter pats	4	case	14.55	case	58.20
TOTAL					$607.31

Page ___ of ___

When each line has been extended, the page is totaled. When each page has been totaled, then all pages are totaled to give the complete inventory figure. In cases where the inventory is categorized, then a total is calculated for each category. *Exhibit 6h* shows an extended inventory for the dairy category.

The totals for all categories are then totaled to arrive at the entire inventory figure. Notice in the example below that the extended inventory value for dairy is added to the totals for the other categories.

Meat	**$ 4,375**
Dairy	**607**
Produce	**780**
Bakery	**250**
Groceries	**3,770**
Supplies	**1,435**
Total	**$ 11,217**

This number is the ending inventory for the operation for that period. It is used in figuring the cost of food sold and inventory turnover. It is also the beginning inventory for the next period.

Think About It...

Bar code scanners are used to automate data collection by translating patterns into information. They also make it easier to track inventory. How would you influence your operation to invest in this type of application?

Software Applications

There is software available for taking, pricing, and extending inventory. At the present time, it is limited to larger operations, primarily due to the cost of the system. The inventory portion of the software is tied into the general accounting process so when goods are received and entered into the system, the price of those goods is transferred to the inventory software. In those operations with inventory software, the person taking inventory passes a handheld bar code scanner over the bar code of the product and enters the count on a keypad. The software recognizes the product by its bar code and retrieves the product's price. The software then takes the count entered on the keypad, extends the price for that product, and totals the inventory. The software can be programmed to use any of the pricing methods previously discussed.

Activity

Inventorying the Produce Section

You have recently been promoted to assistant manager of the Miller Grill Restaurant and the restaurant manager has asked you to complete the inventory of the produce area. He wants you to extend the inventory so that a total inventory for all categories in the storeroom can be made. Put your findings in the produce area in the table below.

1 Extend the listing of items and arrive at a total for the produce area.

Physical Inventory for Miller Grill Restaurant				
Category: Produce	**Date:**		**Counted by:**	**Recorded by:**
Item	**Count**	**Unit**	**Price**	**Total**
Corn, whole kernel	5	#10 can	5.35	$
Cranberry sauce	4	#10 can	8.15	$
Mushrooms, whole	2	#10 can	10.25	$
Peaches, halves	3	#10 can	4.75	$
Pineapple, crushed	6	#10 can	4.85	$
Tomato, purée	6	#10 can	3.50	$
Tomato, whole peeled	5	#10 can	3.45	$
TOTAL				$

2 What is the ending inventory for the produce area? _____

Inventory and the Cost of Food Sold

In Chapter 2, you learned the formula for cost of food sold:

$$\left(\text{Opening inventory} + \text{Purchases} = \text{Total food available} \right) - \text{Closing inventory} = \text{Cost of food sold}$$

Inventory is an integral part of this formula. Only with an accurate inventory will the true cost of food be known. Product inventory must be counted, priced, extended, and totaled correctly. Remember that the opening inventory is the same figure as the closing inventory from the previous period. Note that when closing inventory goes up, cost of food sold goes down. Conversely, when closing inventory goes down, cost of food sold goes up.

Some managers will use this fact for an illegitimate gain, particularly if there is a bonus connected to meeting a standard food cost. If the cost of food sold on the income statement is not up to standard, they will illegally add dollars to the closing inventory to bring the cost of food sold down to the company standard. This activity is known as padding the inventory. **Padding** is the inappropriate activity of adding a value for nonexistent inventory items to the value of total inventory in an effort to understate actual costs. Padding is illegal in many states and in some cases, is against federal law. Regardless of its illegality, it is highly unethical. It is also easy to catch. If the closing inventory is padded, then the opening inventory of the following month is also inflated. This means that for the food cost to meet standard for the next month, the closing inventory must be padded again even more. It will not take management long to discover the deception and terminate the dishonest manager, who will then have a hard time finding other employment. The effective manager will determine why the standard food cost is not being met and take steps to correct the problem.

Inventory Turnover

Inventory turnover is a measure of how quickly an item in storage is used. It is an important number for management to monitor. As was discussed earlier, an operation should have adequate supplies on hand to serve the customer yet not so much as to tie up cash in inventory. An operation with a high inventory turnover rate may not have adequate supplies on hand to produce all of the items listed on the menu at all times. On the other hand, an operation with a low inventory turnover rate will have excess cash tied up and will also have a higher spoilage rate, which will contribute to a high food cost.

Inventory turnover is also important for the independent restaurateur who wants to borrow money from a bank. Inventory turnover is the number one consideration that banks use in their evaluation of a business when making loans.

Figuring inventory turnover is a two-step process. If a foodservice operation has an opening inventory of $8,500, a closing inventory of $10,750, and a cost of food sold of $10,200, the inventory turnover rate can be determined as follows.

1 First, determine average inventory.

$$\frac{\text{Opening inventory} + \text{Closing inventory}}{2} = \text{Average inventory}$$

$$\frac{\$8,500 + \$10,750}{2} = \$9,625$$

2 Then, use the average inventory to get the inventory turnover rate.

$$\frac{\text{Cost of food sold}}{\text{Average inventory}} = \text{Inventory turnover rate}$$

$$\frac{\$10,200}{\$9,625} = 1.06 \text{ Inventory turnover rate}$$

An inventory turnover rate of 1.06 means that the inventory turned over once during this period. Remember, this is the total inventory. As discussed earlier, perishables should be purchased daily or at least every two or three days, while food staples should be purchased weekly. Therefore, during a week, perishables may have turned over several times while nonperishables may have sat on the shelf for a month or more. Inventory turnover rate is an average. An operation that uses more perishables than nonperishables should have a higher turnover rate than an operation with a menu concentrating on nonperishables.

Inventory turnover rate can be calculated for any period: weekly, monthly, or annually. For comparison purposes, it is normally calculated on a weekly basis. But if a restaurant took inventory on a monthly basis, it would figure the inventory turnover rate on a monthly basis and divide the results by 4.3 (the average number of weeks in a month) to get its weekly turnover rate.

The general rule of thumb in the restaurant and foodservice industry is that inventory should turn over one to two times per week. Another rule of thumb is that food inventory should equal one and one-half times the weekly food cost. Thus, if a restaurant has a weekly food cost of $5,000, its average food inventory should be $7,500. As with all guidelines, there can be exceptions. Frequency of delivery, storage and refrigeration space, availability of capital, and menu items all influence how much inventory should be on hand. For example, a restaurant in a metropolitan area that specializes in fresh salads would have a higher inventory turnover rate than a hospital foodservice located in a rural area. However, for the most part, inventory turnover should be maintained within the one to two times per week range.

Activity

Calculating Inventory Turnover Rate

Calculate the inventory turnover rate for an operation, using these numbers.

1 Opening inventory: $20,150
   Closing inventory: $18,950
   Cost of food sold: $24,300
   What is the inventory turnover rate? _____

2 Opening inventory: $12,750
   Closing inventory: $10,500
   Cost of food sold: $14,050
   What is the inventory turnover rate? _____

3 Opening inventory: $27,850
   Closing inventory: $24,350
   Cost of food sold: $32,100
   What is the inventory turnover rate? _____

Perpetual versus Physical Inventory

The discussion so far regarding inventory has revolved around a physical inventory. It is called physical because it is actually physically seen, counted, priced, extended, and totaled. Another type of inventory is perpetual, or theoretical (as discussed on p. 94). That is, it exists on paper only. A perpetual inventory is an excellent storeroom control, but because of the high cost of maintaining a perpetual inventory, its use is limited to larger operations, usually ones with multiple outlets. A large hotel with several restaurants and a banquet department or a large employee foodservice complex with several dining rooms or cafeterias would use perpetual inventory systems. In such operations, it is important for management to know exactly what the food cost is in each of its units. The perpetual inventory system gives them this information.

In these operations, product is purchased by a buyer or purchasing agent for all the units. The food and supplies are delivered to a central storeroom. Each unit then requisitions product from the central storeroom for use in its own kitchen. As a rule, only the product that is needed for that day is requisitioned. The person needing the product fills out the requisition and the department manager or chef approves it. In addition to requisitions, transfers are sometimes used. A **transfer** is a form used to track items going from one foodservice unit to another. For example, the chef may need some wine for cooking and transfer it from the bar. Conversely, the

Exhibit 6i

General Requisition Form

Requisition

Date: _____ Charge to: _____ Department: _____

Requisition approved by: _____

Requisition filled by: _____

Amount	Item	Cost	Extension

bar may need a jar of olives for martinis and transfer these from the main kitchen. *Exhibit 6i* shows a general requisition form that would be used for this type of transfer.

Because the outlying units of a restaurant carry little or no inventory, a daily food cost is needed. **Daily food cost** is an estimate of cost based on requisitions, transfers, and sales. To determine this cost, the daily requisitions for that unit are totaled. Transfers from that unit to another unit are subtracted and transfers into the unit are added to the requisition total to determine the daily food cost for that unit. This number is divided by the unit's sales to determine a daily food cost percent.

Requisitions + Transfers in − Transfers out = Daily food cost

Daily food cost ÷ Unit sales = Daily food cost %

While this is an estimated food cost, it is usually quite accurate since most, if not all, of the food brought into a unit is used that day, hence there is little, if any, inventory on hand.

In addition to figuring the daily food cost for each of the units, a check and balance can be run on the main storeroom. When product is purchased from suppliers and received into the main storeroom, it is recorded on a perpetual inventory sheet and added to the inventory already on hand in the storeroom. (See *Exhibit 6j* on the next page.) When product is requested from one of the units on a requisition form, the storeroom manager subtracts the requested product from inventory on the perpetual inventory sheet. The balance that is shown indicates how much product is on the shelf at all times.

When a physical inventory is taken at the end of the month, it is compared to the perpetual inventory. This comparison is often called actual value versus book value. A variance means that food is missing from the storeroom. The reason for the missing items could be theft,

Exhibit 6j

Sample Perpetual Inventory Sheet

Perpetual Inventory

Item: Sliced peaches   Unit: #10   Par Stock: 12 cans

Date	Start	Received	Issued	Ending	Unit Price	Total
12/05/06	8	0	1	7	$ 5.00	$ 35.00
12/06/06	7	0	0	7	5.00	35.00
12/07/06	7	6	2	11	5.00	55.00
12/08/06	11	0	2	9	5.00	45.00
12/09/06	9	0	1	8	5.00	40.00
12/10/06	8	6	1	13	5.00	65.00

spoilage, or inaccurate bookkeeping. The reason needs to be found and the inventory needs to be corrected, since food missing from the storeroom means that the food cost for that operation has just increased and profit has decreased.

Summary

Goods in storage are as vulnerable to loss as in any other stage of the process from purchasing to service. The two main causes of loss in storage are spoilage and theft. The storeroom must be kept secure, but not to the point of impeding sales. In addition, goods must be rotated properly, kept at the correct temperature, and turned over frequently to prevent spoilage.

Keeping track of the food in storage or inventory is an important part of the control process in restaurant or foodservice operations. Inventory is an operation's control device to help management determine if product that has been received and paid for is actually being used by the kitchen staff and turned into meals that are sold. By knowing the inventory figure, the manager can calculate the cost of food sold, which is management's report card. The cost of food sold tells management if the menu is priced correctly, if the controls in place are working, and how profitable the operation will be. Management also uses cost of food sold to calculate inventory turnover, a control device that tells how fast product in the storeroom is being converted into sales. An additional control point that some operations use is the comparison of physical inventory with perpetual (or theoretical) inventory, which can tell management exactly how much loss is occurring due to spoilage and storage techniques.

Knowing how to prevent and control storage problems and understanding why storage controls are an integral part of the inventory process are vital to the success of any restaurant or foodservice manager.

Activity

Inventory Request

You are the owner-operator of A Wok in the Park, a quick-service Chinese take-out restaurant located across the street from a major metropolitan park. You have contracted with a new accountant to do your books. She has requested the following information from you:

☐ Opening and closing inventory from July

☐ Cost of food sold in dollars for July

☐ Cost of food sold in percent for July

☐ Inventory turnover rate for July

You rummage through your cluttered desk and find the following:

☐ Closing inventory for June was $2,454

☐ Closing inventory for July was $3,105

☐ July purchases were $11,775

☐ July sales were $35,890

This is all the information you can find. From this list of information, supply the accountant with the needed information:

1 Opening inventory for July   _____

2 Closing inventory for July   _____

3 Cost of food sold in dollars for July   _____

4 Cost of food sold in percent for July   _____

5 Inventory turnover rate for July   _____

Then answer the following questions:

6 Is the turnover rate respectable or substandard? Why do you think it is one or the other?

_____

_____

7 If you were the manager of this restaurant, which method of inventory valuation would you use? Why?

_____

_____

Review Your Learning

1 FIFO is

  A. a method of stock rotation.

  B. a method of valuating an inventory.

  C. Both A and B

  D. Neither A nor B

2 Choose the phrase that most closely resembles the act of "extending an inventory."

  A. Purchasing more product

  B. Multiplying the unit cost by the number of units

  C. Obtaining the total cost of the inventory

  D. Combining the cost of a product located in the kitchen and the storeroom

3 Stock rotation is primarily a function performed by the

  A. chef.   C. receiving clerk.

  B. kitchen manager.   D. pantry person.

4 Inventory should be taken

  A. with a frequency that corresponds with the income statement.

  B. in the morning before the operation opens.

  C. by the manager.

  D. by the chef.

5 If the lobby coffee and pastry bar had requisitions of $565, transferred in goods of $25, and transferred out goods of $50, its daily food cost would be

  A. $490.   C. $565.

  B. $540.   D. $640.

6 Given an opening inventory of $8,885, a closing inventory of $12,000, and a cost of food sold of $11,450, what would the inventory turnover for this restaurant be?

  A. 0.90   C. 1.10

  B. 1.05   D. 1.29

7 An inventory that is counted, recorded, priced, extended, and totaled is a

  A. perpetual inventory.   C. physical inventory.

  B. theoretical inventory.   D. A and B only

The following data on inventory pricing for tomato juice applies to questions 8–10.

  i. Opening inventory is 3 cases at $14.00 per case

  ii. Purchases

      a. 4 cases at $14.50

      b. 5 cases at $15.00

8 Using the LIFO method of inventory pricing, the cost per unit on the inventory sheet would be

  A. $14.00.   C. $14.58.

  B. $14.50.   D. $15.00.

9 Using the FIFO method of inventory pricing, the cost per unit would be

  A. $14.00.   C. $14.58.

  B. $14.50.   D. $15.00.

10 Using the averaged price method, the cost per unit would be

  A. $14.00.   C. $14.58.

  B. $14.50.   D. $15.63.

Controlling Food Cost in Production

7

After completing this chapter, you should be able to:

- Develop a food production chart.
- Describe how a waste report helps control food costs.
- Use a conversion factor to calculate a new yield for an existing recipe.
- Determine a recipe's yield and the number of portions it will produce.

Test Your Knowledge

1. **True or False:** Lack of controls in a production kitchen can contribute to increased food cost. *(See p. 110.)*

2. **True or False:** Cooks should be allowed some degree of latitude if they can make a recipe taste better. *(See p. 111.)*

3. **True or False:** If a standardized recipe calls for fifty servings, then fifty servings should be produced, regardless of the sales forecast. *(See pp. 112–113.)*

4. **True or False:** The number of portions a recipe will yield can be calculated by adding the volume or weight of key ingredients and dividing that number by the portion size. *(See p. 122.)*

5. **True or False:** The principal causes of increased food cost in the kitchen are overproduction and not following standardized recipes. *(See p. 110.)*

6. **True or False:** One of the reasons for a taste test is to ascertain the cause of any product flaws. *(See pp. 111–112.)*

7. **True or False:** If a standardized recipe has a yield of 50 portions and 30 portions are needed, the conversion factor would be 1.7. *(See p. 118.)*

8. **True or False:** If a recipe for chili yields 4 gallons and a serving size is 6 ounces, that recipe will yield approximately 85 portions. *(See p. 122.)*

Key Terms

Conversion factor

Food production chart

Recipe conversion

Recipe yield

Taste test

Waste report

Introduction

Like the other segments of an operation, the production area can contribute to increased food costs. The principal causes for this: overproduction by the kitchen and failure to follow standardized recipes. This chapter will examine these causes and provide guidelines to counteract them. The production area must use standards and controls to keep food cost low, just like other areas of the operation. Two of the controls discussed in this chapter are production sheets and standardized recipes.

A manager uses production sheets to determine the number of portions of a given item that the foodservice operation will need on any given day. By following the production sheet, leftovers and waste are reduced, thus keeping food cost in line with the company standards. The use of standardized recipes encourages cooks to use the correct amount of ingredients and also allows for easy recipe conversions. While production sheets and standardized recipes seem compatible, sometimes they are not. Quite often, a production sheet will call for a different amount than the standardized recipe produces. This chapter will introduce how to correct this situation by using recipe conversions.

Every experienced manager knows that most controls do not stand alone. They are all interconnected—the standardized recipe, the menu, the production chart, and the purchasing specifications are interconnected elements that result in food cost that is either under control or not. Managers who know why these production controls are important to monitor and how to calculate the corresponding formulas will increase their effectiveness in ensuring that the production area helps to control food cost.

Exhibit 7a

Management tastes each menu offering to ensure that it meets the operation's standards.

Monitoring the Use of Standardized Recipes

One of the primary duties of managing a foodservice facility is to make sure that the standards and standard recipes of the restaurant are being followed. It should be a daily duty of management to monitor what is happening in the kitchen. (See *Exhibit 7a.*) Cooks often stray from the standard, sometimes out of carelessness and sometimes because they are trying to improve the product. In either case, it is not in the restaurant's best interest to have inconsistent products. Therefore, it is critical that operations use and adhere to standardized recipes.

Taste tests are tastings done prior to the start of a meal period to determine if products meet the restaurant's standards. It should be a daily ritual of management to taste everything on the hot food line as well as all pantry items. When tasting, remember to practice good sanitation by using a different tasting spoon for each item to prevent cross-contamination.

If a product does not meet the standard, it should be pulled from the line and not be served to customers. However, sometimes these items can be salvaged. For example, if some seasonings or a crucial ingredient was not included, sometimes the recipe can be brought up to the standard by adding these ingredients. At other times, the product is a total loss. It could be that the sauce "broke" or that too much of a spice was added and the food item cannot be corrected. In this case, the item should be discarded, which puts management in a lose-lose situation. By throwing the item out, food cost goes up and profit goes down. While wasting food is serious, it is much worse to sell the inferior product and lose customers.

When a product does not meet the operation's standard, management must immediately determine the reason and take corrective action. Some questions that a manager can ask are:

- Is the recipe written clearly?

- Did the cook understand the recipe?

- Are the spices, ingredient bins, packages, and cans clearly labeled?

- Are the appropriate ingredients in the proper containers?

For example, imagine how a chocolate cake might taste if salt were inadvertently put into the sugar bin! After management has determined the cause of the problem, they must take corrective action to avoid having the problem recur.

Determining How Much Food to Produce

While not adhering to standard recipes is a major cause of increased food cost in production, preparing the incorrect amount of product is also a problem. Every operation should strive to produce quantities as close to the quantity actually needed in order to maintain standard food costs and sales. If the operation produces too much food, there will be leftovers. Quite often, these leftovers are not suitable for sale because their appearance and taste do not meet company standards. Sometimes adding leftovers to other recipes, such as adding leftover beef to beef vegetable soup, can salvage the extra product. However, the leftovers rarely bring the same markup as the original product. Conversely, not producing enough product and running out of an item can disappoint customers and runs the risk that they will not return to your establishment. Either of these situations is a lose-lose one for the restaurant. Produce too much and food cost goes up; produce too little and sales are lost. The answer to this dilemma resides in the food production chart.

A **food production chart** is a form that shows how much product should be produced by the kitchen during a given meal period. It is especially useful in foodservice operations where there is a static menu, that is, the same menu day after day. A food production chart can also be used with cycle menus, where the same menu is repeated periodically, depending on the length of the cycle. It cannot be used in an operation where the menu changes daily, such as one where the chef goes to the market and makes up the menu for that day based on what is available. In other words, the menu needs some stability so that a sales history can be developed.

Sales history is critical in helping management forecast how many portions of each menu item to produce on a given day. Management determines what percentage of the total sales each menu item provides. Then management multiplies the percentages by the customer forecast to predict how many portions of each menu item to produce. For example, a restaurant runs these items every Monday on their menu:

- Chicken à la King in a puff-pastry shell

- Roast loin of pork with dressing

- Broiled salmon with lemon butter sauce

- Roast sirloin of beef au jus

- Vegetable lasagna

Having run these items for a while, the restaurant has a sales history. From the sales history, management knows that when this menu runs, the following percentages are sold:

Chicken à la King in a puff-pastry shell	**22%**
Roast loin of pork with dressing	**18%**
Broiled salmon with lemon butter sauce	**15%**
Roast sirloin of beef au jus	**35%**
Vegetable lasagna	**10%**
Total	**100%**

Management can then predict how many customers will come in on that Monday. This calculation is based on past sales history, special events in the areas, weather, and any other pertinent information that could affect sales.

Think About It...

Without historical sales information, how might a restaurant or foodservice organization determine how much of a new menu item to produce?

If 180 customers are expected, then the following portions of each item should be produced:

Chicken à la King in a puff-pastry shell	(180 × .22) = 40
Roast loin of pork with dressing	(180 × .18) = 32
Broiled salmon with lemon butter sauce	(180 × .15) = 27
Roast sirloin of beef au jus	(180 × .35) = 63
Vegetable lasagna	(180 × .10) = 18
Total	**180**

Exhibit 7b illustrates the information that is contained on the production chart for these items. It provides the essential information so that the staff know exactly what and how much to prepare.

Exhibit 7b

Sample Production Chart

DAILY PRODUCTION CHART

				CUSTOMER FORECAST
	WEATHER	EVENTS		180
DAY Monday	DATE 7/28/06	Hot, Dry, 101°	none	

Item	Recipe No.	%	Prepare	Sales	Leftover
Chicken à la King	C–33	22%	40	38	2
Roast loin of pork	P–12	18%	32	29	3
Broiled Salmon	F–48	15%	27	Ran out – 1:10p.m.	0
Roast sirloin of beef	B–8	35%	63	60	3
Vegetable lasagna	V–14	10%	24	20	4

NOTES _____
_____
_____
_____

Not all recipes lend themselves to producing the exact amount predicted. For example, in the above forecast, vegetable lasagna is made in either a full steam table pan or a half pan. A full pan will produce 24 portions while a half pan will produce 12 portions. In this case, management has to decide whether to make a full pan or a half pan. Since 18 portions were predicted, management decided to produce a full pan, which yields 24 portions.

The leftover column on the production chart is important since this could change the percentage of an item over time. Customers' tastes could change or they could react to the latest diet fad and alter their eating habits. Since a production chart is not static, and changes constantly, managers must use good record-keeping to maintain an accurate production schedule.

When the production chart has been completed, it should be posted in the kitchen along with the standardized recipes so that the staff knows exactly how much and which menu items to produce. Managers should periodically conduct recipe yields and check them against the daily production sheet to make sure that the kitchen is producing the proper amount.

Activity

Calculating Portions

Given the following data, determine how many portions of each entrée to produce.

Item	%	Prepare
Baked turkey with cornbread dressing	27%	
Roasted pork tenderloin with apricot glaze	18%	
Blackened redfish	12%	
Roast prime rib of beef	29%	
Macaroni and cheese	14%	
Anticipated number of covers: **470**		

Item	%	Prepare
Firehouse spaghetti	21%	
Parmesan chicken	24%	
Chicken enchilada	15%	
Cha-cha chicken	19%	
Coconut shrimp	21%	
Anticipated number of covers: **380**		

Item	%	Prepare
Grilled shrimp	18%	
Seafood Newburg	26%	
BBQ ribs	22%	
Steak tips linguini	14%	
Beef stroganoff	20%	
Anticipated number of covers: **425**		

Waste Report

Another report that is critical to food cost control in the kitchen is the waste report. As seen in *Exhibit 7c,* the **waste report** is used to track food that was deemed not fit for sale and to list the causes for its waste. A manager has responsibility for reducing waste and maximizing product utilization. The waste report helps a manager track any potential problems and account for unsold merchandise.

Causes of food waste usually fall into two categories: poor training or lack of attention by management. In both situations, employees may feel that a little waste is unavoidable. Management must stress the importance of valuing all products on a daily basis. In addition, the manager must encourage all staff to realize that wasting food not only hurts profits but can ultimately affect their well-being and livelihood through labor cutbacks and other budget cuts that may be implemented to bring overall costs down.

Think About It...

According to numerous statistics, the number of obese Americans is increasing at an alarming rate. Poor nutrition and inactivity are prime causes of this growing trend. How have portion sizes contributed to this trend? How might restaurants help turn this increasing rate around? How could this become a win-win solution for the American public and the food industry?

Exhibit 7c

Sample Waste Report

WASTE REPORT		DATE 7/28/06
FILLED OUT BY Susan Osaki		

Item	Amount	Reason discarded
Peas	5 servings	Too long in steam table
Velouté sauce	1 qt	Sauce broke
Ground beef	20 lb	Not rotated properly
Chicken salad	1 qt	Spoiled, overproduction
Lettuce	4 heads	Rusted

NOTES

Activity

Analyzing a Waste Report

Refer to *Exhibit 7c* and discuss this report in small groups. Answer the following questions:

1 What are your assumptions about the restaurant that generated this report?

_____

_____

_____

_____

_____

2 Look at each line of the report. What went wrong to cause each item's waste?

_____

_____

_____

_____

_____

3 How can each line item's waste be prevented in the future?

_____

_____

_____

_____

_____

4 If you managed this restaurant, would you share this report with your staff? What would you say to them?

_____

_____

_____

_____

_____

Recipe Conversions

As evident from the food production chart in *Exhibit 7b* on p. 114, it is important to produce only what is anticipated to sell. This strategy will help to prevent product outages and will also help to reduce leftovers. In a few cases, such as the lasagna, leftovers cannot be eliminated because of various constraints. However, in most cases, it is possible to produce exactly what is called for on the production chart.

Industry recipes are for portions of 25, 50, or 100. However, if you are using the production charts, you usually do not need portions of 25, 50, or 100. To produce exactly what is needed, the recipe must be converted from its present yield to the desired yield. **Recipe conversion** is a method used to change the yield of a recipe from its original yield to a desired yield. When converting recipes, use a **conversion factor,** or multiplier, to adjust the quantity of ingredients on the existing recipe to the quantity needed to produce the desired yield. The formulas to do this conversion are:

Desired yield ÷ Current recipe yield = Conversion factor

Conversion factor × Current ingredient amount = Desired ingredient amount

When multiplying each ingredient amount by the conversion factor, the ingredient amounts must be in an easily converted form. This means that pounds should be converted to ounces, and that cups, pints, and quarts should be converted into fluid ounces. Teaspoons and tablespoons can be left as is.

To see how a recipe conversion works, follow the steps below to walk through an example of the Chicken à la King from the food production chart in *Exhibit 7b*. In this example, 40 portions are needed. However, the recipe yields 50 portions.

1 Determine the conversion factor by dividing the desired yield by the existing recipe yield.

40 ÷ 50 = 0.8

2 Change the recipe ingredient amounts into ounces (weight) and fluid ounces. (See *Exhibit 7d.*) The new amounts are listed in the third column in the chart.

3 Multiply each ingredient by the conversion factor. In this example, the conversion factor is 0.8. This calculation provides the converted amounts seen in column 5.

4 Convert the ingredient amounts back into the original recipe's amount format. For example, ounces are converted back into pounds and fluid ounces into quarts (see column 6).

Think About It...

Various software solutions can automate recipe conversions and other kitchen functions. What criteria might you use to determine which software to purchase? Research Web sites, such as *www.cheftochef.net* and *www.culinarysoftware.com* to identify available software packages.

Exhibit 7d

Sample Conversion Chart

CONVERSION CHART

ITEM
Chicken à la King

Ingredient	Recipe amount	New amount	Conversion factor	Converted amount	Recipe amount
Chicken, diced	8 lb	128 oz	0.8	102.4 oz	6.25 lb
Butter	1 lb	16 oz	0.8	12.8 oz	0.75 lb
Green pepper, chopped	12 oz		0.8	9.6 oz	10 oz
Mushrooms, sliced	1 lb	16 oz	0.8	12.8 oz	0.75 lb
Pimentos, sliced	14 oz		0.8	11.2 oz	0.75 lb
Heavy cream	3 qt	96 oz	0.8	76.8 oz	2.5 qt
Egg yolks	1 doz	12 each	0.8	9.6 each	10 each
Salt	4 tsp		0.8	3.2 tsp	3 tsp
Sherry	1 qt	32 oz	0.8	25.6 oz	0.75 qt
White pepper	to taste		0.8	to taste	to taste

NOTES

As you can see in the converted amount column (column 5), there can be some unusual numbers. When converting these numbers back into the original units, you must use common sense. For example, the result of converting 12.8 ounces of butter to pounds is 0.8 pounds. Since 0.75 pounds equals ¾ of a pound, 0.8 pounds could be rounded to ¾ of a pound. However, do not make the mistake of converting 0.8 pounds into 8 ounces, or ½ pound. Remember that 0.5 pounds is ½ pound, or 8 ounces.

Obviously, with all of the converting and rounding, the recipe may be changed slightly. When converting recipes, you must use good judgment. For example, hold back some of the spices and taste the product when it is finished, since the spices can always be added later if needed. When converting recipes to smaller yields, such as converting a recipe with a yield of 50 portions to one with 40 portions, there will be little variation in the final outcome. However, problems can arise when converting a small-yield recipe, such as one that produces 50 portions, to a large-yield recipe, such as one that produces 400 portions. In this situation, judgment and experience come into play. For example, one of the reasons that "home" recipes do not always work is due to this extreme conversion factor in large quantities. Whether converting an existing recipe to a smaller yield or a larger one, you will use the same conversion process. In the case of converting to a larger yield, the conversion factor will be greater than 1.0, while in converting to a smaller yield it will be less than 1.0. For example, if 75 portions of Chicken à la King were needed instead of 40, the conversion factor would be 1.5.

Desired yield ÷ Recipe yield = Conversion factor

75 ÷ 50 = 1.5

While recipe conversion works well for most food products, it should be used with extreme caution on baked products. The reason for this caution is that many baked goods rely on chemical reactions that can be affected by heat, moisture, and the amounts of particular ingredients. Because of this situation, the ingredients for most baked products are weighed. When converting weights on baked goods, it is not a good idea to round up or down, but to use the exact weight.

Activity

Converting a Recipe

Complete the recipe conversion chart below for a forecast of 90 portions of Chicken à la King. The original recipe serves 50 portions. Identify the conversion factor and fill in all the empty columns.

Ingredient	Recipe amount	New amount	Conversion factor	Converted amount	Recipe amount
Chicken, diced	8 lb	128 oz			
Butter	1 lb	16 oz			
Green pepper, chopped	12 oz				
Mushrooms, sliced	1 lb	16 oz			
Pimentos, sliced	14 oz				
Heavy cream	3 qt	96 oz			
Egg yolks	1 doz	12 each			
Salt	4 tsp				
Sherry	1 qt	32 oz			
White pepper	to taste				

Activity

Researching and Converting Recipes

You want to add two new salads to your salad bar at the Garden of Eaten in order to take advantage of seasonal produce. First, it is necessary to research the two recipes—one recipe should have cucumbers as its main ingredient and the other should contain blueberries.

Research the recipes online or in the school library. Look for institutional recipes that are written in larger quantities such as 25, 50, and 100.

When you have selected the two new recipes, convert them to a different amount. In other words, if the recipe you selected serves 25 portions, convert it to serve 50 or 60 portions. Enter your information in the charts below.

Cucumber Salad Recipe					
Ingredient	Recipe amount	New amount	Conversion factor	Converted amount	Recipe amount
Recipe name:			Prepared by:		

Blueberry Salad Recipe					
Ingredient	Recipe amount	New amount	Conversion factor	Converted amount	Recipe amount
Recipe name:			Prepared by:		

Determining Recipe Yields

Occasionally, a recipe will not yield the number of portions that it is supposed to yield or a restaurant will opt to serve a different portion size than what is listed on the recipe card. Although management may have determined the standard portion cost for various items on the menu, if the restaurant identifies that the recipes are not producing the number of portions listed, management will need to determine exactly what kind of yield the recipe *is* generating. A **recipe yield** is the process of determining the number of portions that a recipe will produce.

To determine how many portions a recipe yields, calculate the total volume of the recipe either by weight or by volume, depending on how the portion size is calculated. Weigh or measure only the major ingredients. Remember to take cooking loss into account, especially for meat, vegetables, and fruit. For example, to determine the total number of eight-ounce portions available from a macaroni and cheese recipe, you must first look at the recipe's list of ingredients and their volume.

3 lb raw macaroni
2 qt white sauce
2 c grated cheese
4 oz butter
1 tbsp salt
1 tsp paprika
4 oz breadcrumbs

In this particular recipe, only the volume of the macaroni and the white sauce must be calculated. The cheese is not calculated since it is absorbed into the white sauce. Butter, salt, paprika, and breadcrumbs are negligible and also are not counted. Three pounds of raw macaroni yields nine pounds when cooked. Nine pounds converts to 144 ounces (9 × 16 = 144). Two quarts converts to 64 ounces (2 × 32 = 64).

The total volume of the macaroni and cheese recipe is:

144 oz macaroni + 64 oz white sauce = 208 oz product

The total volume is then divided by the portion size to provide the yield of the recipe.

208 oz product ÷ 8 oz portion = 26 servings

Activity

Calculating Recipe Yield

Determine the number of five-ounce portions for the following recipe for corned beef hash. Convert all quantities to ounces before making your calculation.

Corned Beef Hash		
Ingredient	Recipe Quantity	Converted Quantity
Corned beef, cooked and chopped	1½ qt	
Potatoes, cooked and diced	1 qt	
Onions, chopped	½ qt	
Butter	¼ c	
Beef stock	1 qt	
Salt	1 tbsp	
Pepper	to taste	
Parsley, minced	as needed for garnish	

What is the number of portions that this recipe will be able to provide? _____

Calculations:

Activity

Calculating Recipe Yield

You are the owner-operator of the Garden of Eaten, a soup and salad bar restaurant. You found the following recipe for crab bisque in a trade magazine and wish to try it out.

Crab Bisque

- 1 cup roux
- 1 gallon milk
- 1 quart crabmeat
- Salt, to taste
- Pepper, to taste

1 What is the total volume of this recipe?

_____

_____

2 How many 7-ounce portions will the recipe yield?

_____

_____

3 Your mother-in-law thinks that the crab bisque is absolutely fabulous and wants to include it in her garden club's cookbook. Reduce the recipe for her to four 7-ounce portions.

Crab Bisque				
Ingredient	New amount	Conversion factor	Converted amount	Recipe amount
1 c roux				
1 gal milk				
1 qt crabmeat				
Salt, to taste				
Pepper, to taste				

4 Explain to your mother-in-law the pitfalls of reducing a recipe that much.

_____

_____

_____

_____

_____

_____

Summary

One of the primary duties of managing a foodservice facility is to ascertain that the standards of the restaurant are being followed. Two of the primary controls used in the production area— standardized recipes and the production chart—were explained in the chapter. Because not adhering to standard recipes is a major cause of increased food cost in production, management's daily ritual should include taste tests of everything on the hot food line and all pantry items in order to confirm adherence to the standard. When a product does not meet the operation's standard, management must immediately determine the reason and take corrective action. In some cases, food can be salvaged; in other cases it must be discarded. While wasting food is serious and will cause an increase in food costs and a decrease in profits, it is much worse to sell a flawed product and lose customers. Regardless of the reason for the food waste, managers must track the waste on the waste report to identify ways to reduce waste and maximize product utilization.

The second cause of increased food cost is preparing the incorrect amount of product. Every operation should strive to produce quantities as close to the quantity actually needed. If the operation produces too much food, there will be leftovers. Conversely, not producing enough product and running out of an item can disappoint customers and runs the risk that they will not return to the establishment. Either of these scenarios is a lose-lose situation for the restaurant. Many managers use a food production chart to show how much product should be produced by the kitchen for a given meal period. A food production chart is especially useful in foodservice operations where there is a static menu.

Although the food production report states the appropriate amount to produce, some recipes do not yield the needed amount. Managers use two tools to ensure that produced quantity is in line with the food production chart. One tool is recipe conversion, which allows management or food production personnel to change a recipe's original yield to the desired yield. This formula ensures that all of a recipe's ingredients stay in the proper proportion. Occasionally, a recipe does not yield the expected number of portions. In this case, management uses a second tool, recipe yield process, to determine the number of portions that a recipe will produce. Depending on how the portion size is stated, the total volume of the recipe is calculated either by weight or by volume.

Diligently using the controls and tools explained in this chapter will enable you to keep your establishment's food costs in line with your standards.

Review Your Learning

1 A food production chart can be used in operations that have a

  A. static menu.

  B. cycle menu.

  C. menu that changes daily.

  D. A and B only

Data for 2 and 3:

A standardized recipe for lamb stew makes 25 portions. When it runs against other menu items, it accounts for 27 percent of the sales. The prediction for Tuesday is 450 customers.

2 The number of portions that should be produced is

  A. 25.

  B. 112.

  C. 122.

  D. 450.

3 The conversion factor on the standardized recipe should be

  A. 1.

  B. 4.9.

  C. 5.

  D. 6.7.

4 Quiche Lorraine will be served on tomorrow's menu. Each quiche will produce 6 servings. The production chart shows that the anticipated sales are 40 servings. How many quiches should be produced?

  A. 6.

  B. 6.7.

  C. 7.

  D. 7.2.

5 The primary reason(s) for using a production chart are

  A. avoiding leftovers.

  B. meeting customer demand.

  C. Both A and B

  D. Neither A nor B

6 If, after converting a recipe, the amount of an ingredient was 0.9 of a pound, it probably would be rounded to

  A. 8 ounces.

  B. 9 ounces.

  C. 16 ounces.

  D. None of the above

7 If, during a taste test, a product is deemed acceptable, but not up to company standards

  A. it is all right to serve since throwing it out would increase food cost.

  B. it should be sold at a reduced cost.

  C. Either A or B

  D. Neither A nor B

8 A production schedule is based on

  A. knowing the percentage of each item's sales.

  B. predicting the customer count for a given meal period.

  C. Both A and B

  D. Neither A nor B

9 **A waste report**

   A. lists the items in the kitchen deemed unsaleable.

   B. lists the weight of garbage bags going into the dumpster.

   C. lists the income produced by recycling cardboard, plastic, glass, and metal cans.

   D. lists the amount of food left on plates that is not consumed by the customers.

10 **When calculating recipe yield, take cooking loss into account for**

   A. fruit.

   B. vegetables.

   C. meat.

   D. A, B, and C

Notes

Controlling Food Cost in Service and Sales

8

Inside This Chapter

- Service and Portion Control
- Portion Control Devices
- Product Usage Report and Waste Report
- Controlling Food Cost in Sales

After completing this chapter, you should be able to:

- Explain the importance of portion control to food cost.
- Describe various portion control devices and their uses.
- Explain the importance of training, monitoring, and follow-through in portion control.
- Compare the duplicate guest-check system to the POS control system for controlling the receipt of money.
- List the benefits of each payment method used by the restaurant and foodservice industry.
- Describe cash handling procedures used in operations.
- Complete a daily sales report.

Test Your Knowledge

1. **True or False:** The two principal causes of loss in the service function are portion control and theft. *(See p. 131.)*

2. **True or False:** While overportioning will increase food cost, underportioning will lower food cost and is therefore preferable. *(See p. 132.)*

3. **True or False:** In terms of cost control, a preportioned item is preferred over an item that is portioned at service. *(See p. 134.)*

4. **True or False:** A serving scoop is numbered based on how many portions per quart it will yield. *(See pp. 132–133.)*

5. **True or False:** A cup of soup will yield eight ounces. *(See p. 133.)*

6. **True or False:** When using a POS system, each server is issued a set of prenumbered checks at the start of the shift. *(See p. 138.)*

7. **True or False:** Training employees on proper portion control should be done on a weekly basis. *(See p. 134.)*

8. **True or False:** Any time that management is in the kitchen they should be monitoring portion control. *(See p. 135.)*

9. **True or False:** Restaurants that accept credit or debit cards are charged a percentage fee based on the amount of the guest check. *(See p. 140.)*

10. **True or False:** From a restaurant's point of view, both debit cards and credit cards are processed in the same way. *(See p. 140.)*

11. **True or False:** The cashiers should know the sales reading at the end of their shift, so they can balance the cash, checks, and credit/debit cards with the reading. *(See p. 143.)*

Key Terms

Bank

Cash handling procedure

Cash report

Credit card

Daily sales report

Debit card

Duplicate guest-check system

Plate presentation

Point-of-sale (POS) control system

Portion control

Portion control device

Preportioned item

Product usage report

Introduction

The final area to look at in terms of food cost control is the service function. As seen in previous chapters, most of the controls in foodservice interconnect and are dependent on each other. This is why it is so important for management to make sure that each control throughout the process works and is enforced. If one or two controls are missing, there is a strong possibility that food cost will increase.

As you learned in other chapters, mishaps can occur to cause food cost to increase. This chapter will discuss two principal causes of loss in the service area—portion control and theft.

Since the service area consists of the cook's line (also called the chef's line), the pickup line (also called the service line), and the dining room, a myriad of factors can affect getting the proper food served to the customer in the proper amount. During rush periods when stress levels are especially high, portion control can easily get out of hand. Smart management will put into place the many mechanisms and processes to ensure that no matter what shift or time of day it is, portions will not deviate from the standard. The portion control devices discussed in this chapter not only apply to full-service restaurants but also to cafeterias and quick-service operations.

After the food has been served and the customer has finished eating, the customer must pay for the meal. Typically, payment is made either with cash or a credit or debit card. As discussed in a previous chapter, people may try to steal things that are valuable and easy to conceal. This includes cash payments for food served. Therefore, cash control is a very important component of any control system. Common cash control methods are covered in this chapter. These controls will help to ensure that the revenue earned through sales actually shows up in the cash register.

Think About It...

Portions of food are getting bigger and bigger in America. How does portion control affect the bottom line in operations?

Service and Portion Control

The major cost control in service is portion control. **Portion control** is the amount of food in a serving as determined by the standardized recipe or the company standard. This control actually starts with the menu listing. Quite often the menu will list items with their corresponding portion size, such as a "fourteen-ounce strip steak," "six jumbo shrimp," or a "quarter-pound hamburger." These are all examples of portion control. Two important factors need to be kept in mind—the customer often purchases an item based upon its description, and the selling price on the menu is based on the portion being served. If the product is underportioned, the customer may be unhappy and not return. If the product is overportioned, food cost increases and the operation loses money.

Portion control is also linked to the cook's line via the use of standardized recipes. The total amount to prepare is based on the day's anticipated sales for that menu item and the number of portions a recipe produces. For example, management determines that it must prepare twenty-three, eight-ounce servings of macaroni and cheese for the expected lunch crowd today. The standardized recipe for macaroni and cheese requires that the chef cook three pounds of raw macaroni and prepare two quarts of white sauce to prepare twenty-six servings. What would happen to the expected number of servings if the chef put ten-ounce servings on each plate rather than the eight-ounce servings called for in the recipe?

Quite often items are preportioned in a steam table pan for service on the cook's line. A **preportioned item** is food that is measured or weighed prior to going to the service line. Examples of preportioned items are lasagna, Swiss steaks, individual pot pies, and presliced meatloaf. For those items that are not preportioned, there are various tools that can be used to assist in the portioning process.

Whichever method an operation uses for identifying portion size, it is imperative that what is represented on the menu is translated accurately into the standard recipes and then monitored in the serving process to ensure that food cost stays in line.

Portion Control Devices

To assure that the proper portion is being served, there are several implements that can be used. **Portion control devices** are implements that assist in the portioning of food items. They include scoops, ladles, serving spoons, serving dishes, and portion scales.

Exhibit 8a

Number 16 is one-fourth cup.   Number 12 is one-third cup.   Number 8 is one-half cup.

- **Scoops**—These are also known as dishers. (See *Exhibit 8a.*) They are used to portion fluid ounces of semisolid products such as cottage cheese, ice cream, and chicken salad. Scoops are sized and numbered to how many portions the scoop yields per quart. Scoops are numbered from 4 to 40. A number 4 scoop yields four portions per quart, while a number 40 scoop yields forty portions per quart. The most common scoop sizes are 8, 10, 12, 16, and 20; with a number 8 scoop holding one-half cup (four ounces) and a number 20 scoop holding an eighth of a cup (one ounce). The number of the scoop is on the inside of the "blade" that removes the product from the scoop. Quite often, scoops are color-coded on the base of the handle for easy identification by line personnel. Product is portioned correctly when it is level with the top of the scoop.

■ **Ladles**—These devices are used to portion liquid products such as sauces, soups, salad dressings, and entrées with a liquid or sauce base, such as beef stew. They range in size from one-half ounce to eight ounces. Ladles, like scoops, are often color-coded. The size of the ladle is embossed on the top of the handle. (See *Exhibit 8b.*)

■ **Serving spoons**—There are two types of serving spoons, solid and slotted. Solid serving spoons are used for semisolid food items such as macaroni and cheese or mashed potatoes. Slotted spoons are used for products that are in liquid but should be served without the liquid, such as canned vegetables or stewed fruit. A rule of thumb is that one slightly rounded serving spoonful will yield four ounces of product.

■ **Serving dishes**—Many serving dishes also serve as portion-control devices. Even if a serving is overportioned, it will be only slightly overportioned. Some examples are:

   ☐ Ramekins, which are used for sauces or salad dressings. These can vary in size from one ounce to four ounces.

   ☐ Vegetable side dishes, also known as monkey dishes or nappies, are used primarily for vegetables, but can be used for fruit or sometimes sauces. For vegetables, the rule of thumb is that a vegetable side dish will hold four ounces.

   ☐ Individual casseroles, usually round or oblong in shape, typically hold eight to ten ounces of product. This is an excellent way to preportion such items as stews, ragouts, and potpies.

   ☐ Cups and bowls can also be used for portion control. Soup cups and coffee cups are different from an eight ounce measuring cup because they usually hold five to six ounces. A bowl normally holds seven to eight ounces. Some bowls are designed to hold the same amount of product as a cup, yet the charge for a bowl of soup is substantially higher than for a cup of soup. This is a deceptive practice that should not be used by any restaurant.

Exhibit 8b

Ladle sizes are typically stamped on the handle.

■ **Portion scale**—This tool is used for items that are portioned by weight such as roasts, deli meats, and French fries. Portion scales are adjustable so that when a serving plate is placed on the platform, the dial can be adjusted to zero. When the product is placed on the plate, the scale will show the exact weight of the product. The user should make sure that the setting is at zero prior to weighing a product. Portion scales are normally suitable for products weighing zero to thirty-two ounces.

Although some people in the kitchen may believe that they have a "feel" for exact portion sizes, it is important that staff use portion control devices rather than guessing. It is the manager's responsibility to coach employees on the proper use of portion control devices and to insist that employees use them. As managers supervise the kitchen and service lines, they need to monitor and insist on the proper means to ensure portion control.

Preportioning Items

Another mechanism for ensuring that portions are the right size is to preportion any item that can be preportioned before serving. For example, during a rush period, the cook's line can get hectic and errors are more prone to happen. Therefore, preportioning items will not only save time but will also improve accuracy. Deli meats, which can be precut, weighed, and sealed in plastic bags until used for sandwiches are a good choice for preportioning. The more preportioning that can be done, the smoother the rush period will be.

Exhibit 8c

Training and retraining employees in portion control is critical to controlling food cost.

Training

Management spends a good deal of time training employees on the issue of portion control. (See *Exhibit 8c.*) Portion control is not a subject that can be reviewed during employee orientation and then forgotten. Employees have to be constantly trained and retrained to use the portion control devices and to give customers exactly what they are paying for.

There are many reasons for this continuous training, and one important reason is that employees have a tendency to go the extra mile. They want customers to be happy and may feel that giving customers a little extra will make them happier. In some cases, money is involved—employees might believe that a larger portion will secure a larger tip. Whatever the case, management needs to constantly educate their staff. Training in this area is not a day-to-day implementation; it is an hour-to-hour implementation.

Monitoring and Follow-Through

Follow-through is just as important as training. Management needs to constantly check portions to ensure that they are exactly what they should be. For example, if a manager notices a cook cutting steak while the manager is walking through the kitchen, the manager should periodically pick up a steak at random and put it on the portion scale to determine if it is the correct weight. The manager should also do things like check the scoop size used by the pantry person for the tuna salad sandwich, and randomly weigh an order of French fries. If employees know that portion control is a priority with management, they will make it a main concern of theirs.

Plate Presentation

It has been said that customers "eat with their eyes." How a plate looks when it is presented to a customer, whether on a cafeteria line or by a waitperson, is very important. (See *Exhibit 8d*.) **Plate presentation** refers to how an item appears when it is served, including portion, item placement, and garnish. All food must be within the inside rim of the plate. Any sauce that is part of the menu item should be carefully positioned with the item and not dribbled all over the plate. The proper garnish should be placed in the correct position on the plate. Many restaurants have pictures of all entrées displayed in the service area. These pictures depict the proper placement of each item on the plate, its garnish, and the portion to be served. These visual aids ensure that not only will the customer receive an enticing plate, but also one that will be portioned correctly.

Exhibit 8d

Portion sizes in proportion to the plate create the most pleasing plate presentations.

Product Usage Report and Waste Report

In addition to controlling portions in the service procedure, it is important to track some of the more costly items. Two reports are helpful in this regard—the product usage report and the waste report. *Exhibit 8e* has a sample **product usage report,** which shows the number of items issued to the cook's line, the number returned to inventory, and the number sold to customers. The product usage report is often used to track high-cost items such as steak, lobster, and some seafood items. These items are monitored because they are small and expensive, making them conducive to theft. High-cost items should be locked in the walk-in and issued by management to the cook's line prior to a meal period. The amount issued should correspond to a predetermined par stock, which would consist of the average amount needed for a shift plus a safety factor. At the end of the shift, management should tally the number of items left. The amount sold as stated on the product usage report should be compared to the guest checks or the POS printout to determine if any items are missing.

The waste report is also useful in tracking product in the service area. This report was reviewed in Chapter 7 as it applies to production. However, the waste report also has application in the service area. As *Exhibit 8f* shows, this report lists any item that has to be discarded and the reason why. Losses, such as meals returned by customers, dropped trays, items left on the steam table too long, and products that were not up to the restaurant's quality standards are shown on the waste report. By reviewing the waste report, management can track breakdowns in the system and can determine the root causes of these breakdowns, such as preparing too much product in advance, or slippery floors that cause trays to be dropped.

Think About It...

Keeping the money a restaurant earns is every bit as important as *earning* it. In the restaurants where you have worked, what kinds of controls did they use to minimize theft?

Controlling Food Cost in Sales

So far, the focus has been on controlling product from the time it is purchased to the time it is served. Now that the customers have received their meals, management should make sure that what leaves the kitchen is paid for and that the cash is handled properly. Unfortunately, money is the easiest thing to steal in any restaurant or foodservice operation. Consequently, it must be strictly accounted for and the employees entrusted with money must be held accountable for it through tight controls.

Exhibit 8e

Sample Product Usage Report

PRODUCT USAGE REPORT

DATE: 11/16	SHIFT: Dinner	ISSUED BY:	VERIFIED BY: R.B.	RETURNS VERIFIED BY:

Item	Issued	Returned	Sold	Comments
Strip steak (12 oz)	35	5	30	
Rib eye steak (14 oz)	40	2	37	1 ret'd overcooked
Medallions	25	1	24	
Filet mignon	50	6	44	
Lobster tails	40	10	30	

NOTES

Exhibit 8f

Sample Waste Report

WASTE REPORT

FILLED OUT BY:

DATE: Nov. 16

Item	Amount	Reason discarded
Peas	5 servings	Too long in steam table
Velouté sauce	1 qt.	Sauce broke
Rib eye steak (14 oz)	1 serving	Overcooked, returned by customer
Ground beef	20 lb	Not rotated properly
Chicken salad	1 qt.	Spoiled, overproduction
Lettuce	4 heads	Rusted

NOTES

Duplicate Guest-Check and POS Control Systems

The duplicate guest-check system and the point-of-sale (POS) control system are the most widely used methods in the restaurant industry today. The **duplicate guest-check system** is a procedure that uses written records of what guests purchased and how much they were charged for the items. The **POS control system** is a method that uses a computer to ensure that what leaves the kitchen is billed to and paid for by customers. Although both processes are used to monitor, control, and ensure payment for food, the major difference is that in the POS system, technology takes the place of manually writing a guest check. As more restaurants embrace technology, the POS system is rapidly replacing the manual check system.

The steps below outline the duplicate guest-check system. Each guest check is prenumbered and has a duplicate; that is, when the customer's order is written on the first copy of a check, it is also written on the second copy. (See *Exhibit 8g.*)

Exhibit 8g

Duplicate guest check given to the kitchen for order fulfillment

Original guest check given to customer for payment

1 At the start of the shift a set of guest checks is issued to each server. The numbers on the checks are recorded.

2 The server writes the customer's order on the guest check, which copies the order to the second, or duplicate, copy of the guest check. (See *Exhibit 8g.*)

3 The second copy is turned in to the kitchen; the kitchen fills the order and keeps the duplicate. No order leaves the kitchen without the duplicate of a guest check.

4 When the customer has finished eating, he or she is presented with the original check that has been totaled.

5 The customer pays the bill.

6 At the end of the shift, the server checks out. All guest checks, used and unused, must be accounted for.

7 At the end of the shift, management collects all of the duplicates from the kitchen.

8 The bookkeeper matches the originals with the duplicates to see if there are any discrepancies, alterations, or missing checks.

Restaurants have different policies on how to handle missing checks. Some charge the servers a set amount for each missing check while others do not. When setting this policy, note that the Federal Minimum Wage Law prohibits charging employees for mishaps if the charge brings the employee's wages below minimum wage. There are also state laws governing such practices.

Operations that use a POS system function in basically the same way, except there are no prenumbered checks. (See *Exhibit 8h*.) Instead, each server is assigned a code. When the server inputs the customer's order into the system, the order is allocated to that server who is then responsible for it. The order is simultaneously printed in the kitchen. No order should leave the kitchen without a printed directive. When the customer has finished his or her meal, the server prints the check and presents it to the customer who then pays it. When the customer receives his or her change or charge slip to sign, the customer is given a copy of the check.

Exhibit 8h

Similarities and Differences of Duplicate Check and POS Systems

Similarities

- If not careful, server can order incorrect meal with either system
- Both allow for accounting of meals ordered
- Both allow for reconciliation of meals ordered with meals delivered by the kitchen
- Both allow for presentation of meal check to customer

Differences

- POS uses a computer; duplicate check uses paper
- POS system keeps running tally of sales; with duplicate check, sales must be totaled manually or taken from cash register
- Order entry in POS system can automatically track food costs and perpetual inventory; food costs and inventory must be calculated manually when using a duplicate check system.
- Employee-level data, such as covers sold or sales per cover, are easily derived from POS systems. Deriving the same information from duplicate checks is largely a manual effort.
- Some POS systems can display more information for kitchen staff about the dish ordered. In the duplicate check system only the server's notation of the order is displayed.
- In the duplicate check system, kitchen staff must know how to read each server's handwriting and shorthand notes. A POS system displays the order information on a screen or prints out a copy of the order.
- In the duplicate check system, reconciliation of original check and duplicate check must be done by hand. This is done automatically in POS system.

Paying the Check

One of the last steps in either the duplicate guest-check system or the POS control system is for the customer to pay the bill for the food that was served. Restaurant and foodservice operations can accept payment in several forms. Some will use all of these payment options while others will use only some of them. In fact, some operations will accept cash only. The types of payment options used are:

- **Cash**—Universally accepted.

- **Credit card**—Popular form of payment, especially in larger operations and chains. A **credit card** obligates the user of the card to pay their credit card company for the products and services they have charged to the card. There is, however, a cost involved to the restaurant. The bank that issues the card and the credit card company charge the restaurant a fee that is normally a percentage of the guest check. When the guest presents a credit card to the person collecting, it is processed for authorization, which completes the transaction. The cash terminal prints two receipts. The customer keeps one receipt and signs the other. The signed receipt is turned in with the cash proceeds at the end of the day.

- **Debit card**—From the restaurant's point of view, a debit card is processed in the same way as a credit card. However, the main difference is from the customer's standpoint. When using a **debit card,** the amount is immediately withdrawn from the cardholder's bank account. With a credit card, the cardholder pays for the entire amount due at the end of the billing cycle or extends payments and pays interest, much like taking out a loan.

- **Traveler's check**—Accepted because of their safety and the fact that the issuing company normally safeguards them against theft. However, this method is decreasing in popularity and acceptance. There are two signature lines on a traveler's check. One signature line is signed when the check is issued. The second signature line is signed when the check is cashed. The person receiving the check should observe the customer signing the check and then compare the two signatures.

- **Personal check**—Not accepted in many operations due to the possibility of receiving a "bad check." A bad check could be due to nonsufficient funds (NSF), which means the check's bank account did not contain sufficient funds to cover the amount written on the check. A bad check could also be a stolen check. In either case, the check is returned to the operation, which is not paid for the value of the check. Restaurant and foodservice operations that accept checks often pay for a check approval service that will preapprove checks and cover any losses from bad checks. When checks are remitted for payment, they should be stamped on the back "for deposit only" and deposited to the restaurant's account at the end of the day.

- **Other methods**—It is becoming more common for organizations to offer other means of payment, such as corporate accounts, house accounts, vouchers, and comps (complimentary meals). Each organization has their own policies on these methods of payment.

Who Handles Cash?

The person or persons who handle cash in the operation, and how many there are, depend on the type of operation. Each operation may use a different strategy regarding cash handling. Each restaurant category has typical cash handling strategies they use.

- **Quick service**—In quick-service operations, several people could handle cash, depending on business volume. A counterperson takes the customer's order and enters it into the POS system. The order is printed in the kitchen. The counterperson collects money or completes a charge transaction with the customer. In some operations, the same counterperson assembles the order and gives it to the customer. In other operations, a number is printed on the customer's receipt and another counterperson gives the customer his or her order.

- **Cafeteria**—Customers select their own food and then proceed to the cashier's station where they pay prior to going into the dining room. Most cafeterias are cash only, but some accept charge cards. Some commercial cafeterias have a checker who adds up what the customer has selected and gives him or her a receipt that is then paid to a cashier when leaving the premises. Some noncommercial cafeterias, such as college dorms, have no cashiers but operate on a monthly or semester payment plan.

- **Family style**—These operations include hotel coffee shops and truck stops. The cashier collects money for all transactions in the restaurant. These operations normally use the duplicate guest check or POS control system.

- **Casual/Fine dining**—This group of restaurants includes upscale establishments and sports bars as well as bar and grill operations. In these restaurants, the server normally collects from the customer. Servers are responsible for their own checks and turn money and charge receipts in to management at the end of their shift. These operations have no cashier since each server acts as his or her own cashier.

Preventing Skips

On occasion, a customer will leave an establishment without paying for his or her meal. In order to prevent this from occurring, management should teach their staff the following preventive measures:

■ If the custom of your establishment is that guests order and consume their food prior to your receiving payment, instruct servers to present the bill for the food promptly after the guests have finished their meal.

■ If your establishment has a cashier in a central location in the dining area, have that cashier available and visible at all times.

■ If each server collects for his or her own guest's charges, instruct the servers to return to the table promptly after presenting the guest's bill to secure a form of payment.

■ Train staff to be observant of exit doors near restrooms or other facilities which may provide an unscrupulous guest the opportunity to exit the dining area without being seen.

■ Train staff to notify management immediately if they see a guest leave without paying the bill.

■ When approaching a guest who has left without paying the bill, the manager should ask the guest if he or she inadvertently "forgot" to pay the bill.

■ If a guest refuses to pay the bill or flees the scene, the manager should complete an incident report that notes the time and date of the incident, name of server who served the guest, number of guest involved, the amount of the bill, physical description of the guest(s), and vehicle description.

■ If a guest flees the scene, the manager should contact the police. In no case should staff or managers attempt to physically restrain or detain the guest. The liability that could be involved could far outweigh the value of the unpaid dining bill.

Activity

Benefits to Accepting Credit Cards

Divide into three groups. Select one of the major credit cards and research its benefits and services. For each credit card, look at its Web site and find the Merchants section. This section will help you learn more about the credit card's benefits and services.

In your group, prepare a sales pitch that you could use to persuade management to accept this credit card at your restaurant. Present your pitch to the other groups.

After all the pitches are presented, answer the following questions:

1 How do the benefits of each company compare?

_____

_____

_____

_____

_____

_____

_____

_____

2 Which benefits do you think are most important to a restaurant?

_____

_____

_____

_____

_____

_____

_____

_____

3 Which credit card(s) would you choose to accept at a restaurant you managed?

_____

_____

_____

_____

_____

_____

_____

Cash Handling Procedures

Whether a cashier, counter attendant, or server handles the cash transactions in a restaurant or foodservice operation, the procedure is the same. **Cash handling procedures** are the activities that operations follow to ensure that all cash and charge transactions are accurate and accounted for. For the purposes of this discussion, the term "cashier" will be used to describe the employee handling the transaction.

1 A bank is issued to each cashier, or in some operations, to a particular cash register or POS drawer that may be shared by multiple users. A **bank** consists of coins and dollar bills sufficient to make change. The size of the bank is determined by the number of anticipated transactions.

2 The cashier receiving the bank counts and verifies the amount, since he or she is responsible for it.

3 No person other than the cashier should be allowed near the cash register during the cashier's shift. If the cashier leaves for any reason, the drawer should be locked.

4 The cashier collects cash, charges (debit and credit), and checks (if allowed) from the customers.

5 At the end of the shift, a reading is normally taken by management. If a cash register is being used, the readings are locked with only management having a key. The readings are continuous; that is, they continue from shift to shift and are not totaled. Thus, the reading from the current shift has to be subtracted from the previous shift to get the sales for the current shift. If the operation uses a POS system, management enters a code to obtain a reading.

6 The cashier counts the drawer, sets aside the bank, totals the checks and the charges, and fills out a cash report. As shown in *Exhibit 8i,* a **cash report** is a form filled out by the cashier to report all money, checks, and charge slips collected during the shift.

7 Management or a bookkeeper completes a daily sales report (see *Exhibit 8j*) from the cash report and the register readings. A **daily sales report** is a form that shows sales, cash, and charges collected as well as any money over or short for a shift.

Exhibit 8i

Sample Cash Report

CASH REPORT

DATE 06-30-2005   SHIFT PM   LOCATION 54

CASHIER *Tony Andrini*   VERIFIED BY *ML*

ITEM	AMOUNT	EXTENSION	TOTALS
Currency			
$100	0	$ -	
$50	1	$ 50.00	
$20	23	$ 460.00	
$10	47	$ 470.00	
$5	43	$ 215.00	
$2	0	$ -	
$1	244	$ 244.00	
Total currency			$ 1,439.00
Coin			
$1.00	0	$ -	
$0.50	0	$ -	
$0.25	56	$ 14.00	
$0.10	32	$ 3.20	
$0.05	55	$ 2.75	
$0.01	63	$ 0.63	
Total coin			$ 20. 58
Total charge slips			2,489.54
Total checks			127.98
Total turned in			$ 4,077.10
Less: bank			300.00
TOTAL SALES			$ 3,777.10

Exhibit 8j

Sample Daily Sales Report

DAILY SALES REPORT

DATE 06-30-2005   SHIFT PM   LOCATION 54

CASHIER *Tony Andrini*   VERIFIED BY *ML*

Registered reading ending	$	576,382.90
Less: register reading start		572,603.36
= Sales		3,779.54
Currency/coin turned in	$	1,459.58
Checks turned in		127.98
Charges turned in		2,489.54
= Total amount turned in	$	4,077.10
Less: bank		300.00
= Net turned in	$	3,777.10
Sales	$	3,779.54
Less: net turned in		3,777.10
= Difference	$	2.44
Reason: wrong change given		

Notice that the cash report and the daily sales report are done separately and by two different people. In most operations, the cashier does not know what the cash register readings are for the shift. The reason for this is to encourage the reporting of actual results and to discourage theft. Another reason is that the cashier will not always balance at the end of the shift. Most times, there will be overages or shortages; however, they should be minor discrepancies. In fact, management should be suspicious if the cashier balances every time. If cashiers were to complete their cash report to match the cash register readings, poor cash handling techniques or theft would never come to light.

In the system where the server collects the payment from the customer, the server's cash report will always balance. The reason for this is that servers turn in the bank and cash and credit/debit slips for the total of their sales. Any monies left over are their tips.

Whether the cash control is manual or automated, management must understand the importance of implementing procedures like these to ensure that all money is accounted for.

Activity

Figuring the Daily Sales Report

Cathy operates a small, upscale bakery in a quaint resort village in the mountains. Complete the daily sales report for Friday by filling in the blanks below. Then answer the questions following the sales report.

Daily Sales Report		
Date: Friday, September 20	**Location:**	**Shift:**
Prepared by:	**Verified by:**	
Register reading ending	$ 37,532.50	
Less: register reading start	$ 35,475.01	
= Sales	$ 2,057.49	
Currency/coin turned in	$ 1,211.30	
Checks turned in	$ 72.78	
Charges turned in	$ 944.85	
= Total amount turned in	$	
Less: bank	$ 175.00	
= Net turned in	$	
Sales	$	
Less: net amount turned in	$	
= Difference	$	
Reason		

1 What kind of cash control problem does Cathy have?

_____

_____

_____

_____

_____

_____

_____

_____

2 What solutions would you suggest to her to eliminate this problem?

_____

_____

_____

_____

_____

_____

_____

_____

_____

Activity

Theft and Reputation—What Should I Do?

You are the owner of a family-style restaurant in a small town in the Midwest. The economy of the town is dependent primarily on agriculture. Your business has been quite successful because it is the gathering spot for the community. Since you have put in many long hours to get the restaurant to this point, you have decided to slow down a little and work fewer hours.

You decide to hire a night manager to supervise the evening shift. He is a local farmer who is down on his luck at the moment and needs the extra income. It looks like the ideal situation for him since he can farm during the day and work for you in the evening. He is well known in town, belongs to a local civic group, and serves on the board of the Chamber of Commerce. You figure he would be good for your business, since he already knows most of your customers.

After a few months, you notice that evening sales are dropping. Being concerned, you drop in unexpectedly for a few nights. Things appear to be fine. The restaurant is full and customers are getting good service and good food.

There are few controls in the restaurant since you were there most of the time and did not see any reason to do extra paperwork. On one of the evenings, a trusted employee tells you that the night manager is stealing. You decide to put some extra money in the cash register to see what happens. The next day, there is no overage reported. You confront the night manager. He admits to stealing money to pay bills.

You now have to make a decision on what to do about this situation. If you terminate him, his reputation in this small town may be ruined. Or there could be a backlash and people might stop coming into your restaurant because you fired a popular citizen. On the other hand, at least one of your employees knows the night manager has been stealing from you, and if you do not terminate him, your staff could assume it is all right to steal.

In small groups, discuss the following questions:

1. As the owner of the restaurant, what should you do?

_____

_____

2. How would you handle the consequences with the public? With your staff?

_____

_____

3. How could this situation have been prevented?

_____

_____

Summary

Management must be extremely vigilant in the service area to control food cost. Two of the greatest threats are overportioning and theft of cash. Every item served, no matter how small, should have a correct portion assigned to it by management. This chapter reviewed the various portion control devices that can be utilized to ensure that portion-size standards are met. The chapter also discussed the importance of supervising employees to ensure correct portioning, and the importance of continuous training and follow-through, which can increase the success of your control process.

A variety of reports, such as the waste report, cash report, and daily sales report, can help management pinpoint areas in need of additional cost control. These reports can also aid management in finding the root cause of cost control problems within the organization.

Two different methods of controlling cash in sales were described. One is a manual system of duplicate guest checks, while the other is a POS control system that involves the use of technology. More and more operations are moving toward the use of automated computer systems to manage this area of sales. However, management must remember that simply adding technology to the process will not ensure a good control system. Such a system must be designed effectively and used properly by managers and staff.

In addition, a cash control system must be in place in all operations. As part of this process, servers should be responsible for their assigned checks and for monies collected. Various cash handling procedures can be used, depending on the operation. When the time comes to check the daily sales, two or more staff members should be responsible for checking it against the daily receipts. Given the threat of theft in the cash handling process, this area of the operation should be supervised more closely than others.

Review Your Learning

1 A number 8 scoop will yield

A. eight servings per quart.

B. one-half cup of product.

C. Both A and B

D. Neither A nor B

2 On the average, a slightly rounded serving spoon will yield

A. three ounces of product.

B. four ounces of product.

C. five ounces of product.

D. six ounces of product.

3 A ramekin is used for

A. individual casseroles.

B. sauces or salad dressings.

C. vegetables.

D. soup.

4 A cup used to serve soup will hold

A. three to four ounces.

B. four to five ounces.

C. five to six ounces.

D. seven to eight ounces.

5 Proper plate presentation includes

A. portion control.

B. a neat-looking plate with all product inside the rim.

C. a proper garnish.

D. All of the above

6 Monitoring high-cost items, such as steak and seafood, on the cook's line is best done by

A. establishing a par stock for those items and issuing that amount prior to the start of a shift.

B. using a product usage report.

C. Both A and B

D. Neither A nor B

7 In the duplicate guest-check system, the guest checks turned in by the cashier and the copies from the kitchen are matched by

A. the bookkeeper.

B. the cashier.

C. a member of the waitstaff.

D. the dining room manager.

8 The system where the server collects, and is responsible for, all the money and credit card transactions he or she handled is normally found in

A. cafeterias.

B. truck stops.

C. hotel coffee shops.

D. sports bars.

9 Cash register readings at the end of the shift are normally taken by the

A. management.

B. cashier.

C. bookkeeper.

D. greeter.

continued on next page

Review Your Learning *continued from previous page*

10. Training employees on portion control is best done

    A. during employee orientation.
    B. at weekly meetings of the kitchen staff.
    C. daily.
    D. hourly.

11. A portion scale should be used to portion

    A. salad dressing.
    B. French fries.
    C. Irish stew.
    D. mashed potatoes.

12. High-cost items, such as steak, should be tracked using a

    A. product usage report.
    B. physical inventory.
    C. waste report.
    D. sales report.

13. To make sure that everything leaving the kitchen gets paid for, the most popular system(s) in use today is/are

    A. the duplicate guest-check system.
    B. the POS control system.
    C. Both A and B
    D. Neither A nor B

14. If a server who was issued guest checks at the start of the shift has some missing,

    A. management can deduct a set amount for each missing check from the server's pay.
    B. the deduction cannot bring the server's pay below the Federal Minimum Wage Law.
    C. management cannot deduct anything from the server's pay according to federal law.
    D. A and B only

Controlling Labor Costs

9

After completing this chapter, you should be able to:

- Distinguish between fixed, variable, and semivariable costs.
- Explain how payroll cost, FICA, Medicare, and employee benefits make up labor cost.
- Describe the components and factors to consider in the development of a master schedule.
- Explain the difference between a master schedule and a crew schedule.
- List factors that affect labor cost.
- Explain how direct factors, such as business volume, affect labor cost.
- Calculate turnover rate percentage, total dollars for labor costs, dollars available for scheduling, and hours available for scheduling.
- Explain how indirect factors, such as quality and productivity standards, affect labor costs.

Test Your Knowledge

1 **True or False:** If more dollars were spent in February than in January, then February's labor cost would inevitably be higher. *(See pp. 153–154.)*

2 **True or False:** Budgets are normally prepared in the form of a pro forma income statement. *(See p. 157.)*

3 **True or False:** To calculate the dollars available for labor cost, multiply the projected sales by the standard labor cost percent. *(See p. 160.)*

4 **True or False:** When placed on the schedule, hourly employees become fixed-cost employees. *(See p. 161.)*

5 **True or False:** To determine the number of hours available to schedule, divide the payroll dollars available by the average wage per hour. *(See pp. 163–164.)*

6 **True or False:** Employee turnover is a major problem in the foodservice industry. *(See p. 169.)*

7 **True or False:** Some employee benefits could be offered to management, but not to hourly employees. *(See p. 172.)*

8 **True or False:** To calculate a labor cost percent, divide sales by labor cost. *(See p. 156.)*

9 **True or False:** If an employee is working and is not on the schedule, he or she should not clock in. *(See p. 169.)*

10 **True or False:** So that paying overtime can be avoided, an employee should be instructed to work off the clock and be given paid time off at a later date. *(See p. 169.)*

11 **True or False:** Job descriptions are a key instrument when enforcing quality and productivity standards. *(See p. 173.)*

Key Terms

Budget	Job description	Overtime
Covers per server	Labor contract	Payroll dollars
Crew schedule	Labor cost	Person-hour
Employee benefits	Labor cost percent	Productivity standard
Employee turnover	Master schedule	Quality standard
Federal Insurance Contributions Act (FICA)	Medicare	Return chart

Introduction

Along with food costs, labor costs consume the greatest portion of a restaurant or foodservice organization's revenue. Because of their impact on profits, managers must be able to use various methods to control labor costs to the extent possible. However, labor is a very difficult cost to control for two reasons. One is that you are dealing with people—their personalities, their ability to work with others, their productivity and quality of work, and their individual personal problems. A manager must deal with and leverage all these factors when creating a work schedule.

The second reason is that the future is unknown. When scheduling employees, the manager does not know what future sales will be, nor how many employees will actually be needed. While a manager strives to make an accurate sales projection, unforeseen events can occur and lead to sales increasing or decreasing. With scheduled staff being a variable expense, the labor cost is reflected in these sales fluctuations. Management must be able to make adjustments quickly so that labor cost does not get out of line. This chapter will explain how to establish and follow labor controls, including instructions for setting up a master schedule and creating a crew schedule. In addition, this chapter will explore other direct and indirect factors that can affect labor costs.

Exhibit 9a

Payroll Costs versus Sales

Variable payroll costs change in direct proportion to sales, while fixed payroll costs do not.

Labor Costs

You might recall from Chapter 1 that costs are divided into three categories—fixed, variable, and semivariable. Fixed costs are those costs that stay the same regardless of sales volume. Variable costs are costs that increase and decrease as sales increase or decrease and do so in direct proportion. Semivariable costs are costs that increase and decrease as sales increase and decrease, but not in direct proportion. The reason for the lack of a direct relationship with a semivariable cost is that this type of cost is made up of both fixed costs and variable costs. Payroll and labor are good examples of a semivariable cost—both consist of fixed and variable costs. (See *Exhibit 9a.*)

Exhibit 9b

Labor is considered a semivariable cost because it has a fixed component (salaried employees), as well as a variable component (hourly employees).

Payroll Cost

Often the terms *labor cost* and *payroll cost* are used interchangeably in the restaurant industry. They are, in reality, two different things. Payroll cost is the amount of money that is spent for employee wages, both fixed and variable. The fixed payroll cost is usually management salaries. Management, for the most part, is paid a salary that remains the same regardless of the restaurant's sales volume. For example, if the general manager's salary is $70,000 per year, that is the amount the general manager would receive, regardless of whether the restaurant brought in $1,000,000 or $1,300,000 per year. Thus, management payroll cost is a fixed cost.

On the other hand, the waitstaff, line cooks, and dishwashers are paid an hourly wage and are scheduled according to anticipated sales. For example, more staff is scheduled at peak sales times than at slower sales times. As a consequence, staff payroll costs are higher during peak sales times than they are at slower sales times. Since staff payroll costs increase or decrease in proportion to sales, staff payroll cost is a variable cost.

Combining the fixed management payroll cost with the variable staff payroll cost results in a semivariable payroll cost. This semivariable payroll cost increases as sales increase and decreases when sales decrease but not in direct proportion with sales. (See *Exhibit 9b.*)

Labor Cost Includes Payroll and Employee Benefits

Labor cost, as expressed on the income statement, is much more than the amount of money spent on management salaries and employees' hourly wages. **Labor cost** is all-inclusive and includes, in addition to payroll cost, such costs as the employer's contribution to FICA and Medicare, worker's compensation insurance, and employee benefits. All of these are integral parts of labor cost and should be calculated into the labor cost total. It is also important to distinguish that payroll cost is the gross (pay before taxes are deducted), not net, total of the paychecks.

The **Federal Insurance Contributions Act (FICA)** is a program for retirement and medical benefits administered by the federal government and paid for by employers and employees. This program sets money aside for Social Security payments. The current contribution rate is 6.2 percent, which means that every employee contributes 6.2 percent of his or her gross pay for FICA and each employer contributes 6.2 percent of gross pay for each of their employees. Likewise, a contribution to **Medicare**—money set aside for health benefits for those who cannot afford them— is 1.5 percent. Combined, the two taxes total 7.7 percent. When figuring FICA and Medicare contributions for payroll expenses, only the employer's share is figured, since that is the only expense for the employer. The employee's share is paid by the employee.

Another labor cost to take into consideration is unemployment insurance, which is required by the federal government but is implemented by the states. Unemployment insurance is funded through payroll taxes paid by employers. The amount of this tax varies by state and by employer. For example, if an employer has terminated or laid off many employees who filed for unemployment benefits, that employer's tax rate will be higher compared to employers who have not had as many claims.

Employee benefits vary widely from company to company. **Employee benefits** are employment benefits given by an employer that have monetary value but do not affect the basic wage rate. Employers may offer all, some, or none of the following:

- Paid holidays
- Paid vacation
- Paid sick days
- Health insurance

- Life insurance
- Dental insurance
- Company-paid retirement plans

Adding payroll costs, employer's FICA contribution, employer's Medicare contribution, and the costs associated with employee benefits, gives management the total labor cost.

The Relationship Between Labor Cost and Business Volume

Although total labor costs might be a large number, management is most concerned about the relationship between labor cost and sales. When comparing a cost to sales volume, the manager must convert the cost into a percentage of sales. To simply look at the dollars spent is to see only part of the picture. For example, suppose that a restaurant spent more labor dollars in July than in June. By merely looking at the dollars spent, the manager would not be able to easily determine if this increase in labor cost indicates a problem or not.

Think About It...

Offering employee benefits can cost an employer up to 50 percent of payroll costs. Of the benefits an employer can offer, which are the benefits you find most desirable? What are some ways employers can reduce benefit costs but still offer desirable benefits to employees?

However, by converting labor costs in June and July to a percentage of sales, the manager would be better able to determine if corrective action is needed. By looking at labor cost as a percentage, the relationship between labor cost and sales is taken into account.

To calculate **labor cost percent,** which is the relationship between labor cost and business volume, divide the actual labor cost by sales as shown in the following formula:

Labor cost ÷ Sales = Labor cost percent

For example, if a restaurant's sales are $12,000 for a week and the labor cost is $4,000 for the same week, then the labor cost percent for that week is 33.3 percent.

$4,000 ÷ $12,000 = .333 or 33.3%

Labor cost percent can be calculated for any period of time, but is normally calculated for a week, month, or year.

While most operations look at labor cost percentage monthly, many also analyze it daily by using a calculation for the estimated daily payroll cost percentage:

1 Divide the weekly fixed cost (management's salaries) by seven (assuming the restaurant is open seven days a week) to get the daily fixed payroll cost.

Weekly management salaries ÷ 7 days = Daily fixed payroll cost

2 Add the daily fixed payroll cost from Step 1 to the variable payroll cost for hourly employees to get the total daily payroll cost. The variable payroll cost is taken from the master schedule.

Daily fixed payroll cost + Daily variable payroll cost = Total daily payroll cost

3 Divide the total daily payroll cost from Step 2 by the anticipated sales for that day to get the estimated daily payroll percent. Compare this daily payroll percent figure to the operation's standard labor percent.

Total daily payroll cost ÷ Anticipated daily sales = Estimated daily payroll cost percent

While the estimated daily payroll cost percentage is not as accurate as a weekly or monthly labor cost percentage, it gives management a picture of whether the operation is on budget for payroll cost. If the cost is out of line, management can take immediate action to correct the problem. Action taken immediately can help ensure that the weekly or monthly payroll is within budget. Without taking a daily reading on labor cost, management could be unpleasantly surprised when the month-end report is prepared.

Budget as a Cost Control

When it comes to controlling costs, it is easy to spend more than intended. This is especially true of labor cost, because it is one of the highest costs an operation has. Having a budget helps managers plan the financial activities related to their daily operations. A **budget** is a projection of sales, costs, and profit that is used to guide day-to-day operational decisions. It is also used to create the master schedule.

Budgets are created based on historical figures and educated forecasts of what will happen to sales and costs in a specific period. These are projected on a monthly basis and totaled to a yearly figure.

The amount allocated for labor is dependent on several factors:

- Menu items
- Level of expertise needed to execute the menu items
- Method and amount of preparation needed
- Type of service
- Location
- Special events or holidays

In addition, management takes into account any actions that may cause an increase in cost. For example, if a union contract that covers the hourly employees will expire next year, management would likely forecast an increase in the hourly rate paid to staff. Consequently, the labor cost would increase when calculating next year's budget.

While budgets are basically an estimate of what will happen in the future, if they are carefully done, they are an accurate guideline to assist the manager in achieving profitability.

The Budget's Relationship to Standards

Budgets are normally generated in the form of a pro forma income statement. (See *Exhibit 9c.*) That is, they show sales, all costs, and profit. Each line is shown in dollars as well as percentages.

Exhibit 9c

Sample Pro Forma Income Statement

Pro Forma Income Statement
Slippery Noodle Restaurant

Sales	$ 1,450,000	100%
Cost of food sold	− 493,000	34%
Gross profit	$ 957,000	**66%**
Labor expenses	$ 420,500	29%
Other controllable expenses	93,000	6%
Noncontrollable expenses	+ 330,000	23%
Total expenses	$ 843,500	**58%**
Profit	$ 113,500	8%

157

For an operation to achieve its budgeted profit, the sales projections listed in its budget must be met. Additionally, the operation's costs must be held to their standards, which is the budgeted dollar amount or percentage for each type of cost.

It is an important part of the management function to make sure that payroll cost is in line with the budgeted standard. If the cost goes below the standard, the quality of food or service could suffer, resulting in lost sales. If the cost is above the standard, the profit will suffer. The first step in assuring that labor cost will meet the standard is the creation of a work schedule.

Creating Schedules

Payroll controls and the budget start with the schedule. To have a successful control, a plan is needed. The plan starts with a master schedule based on projected sales that are, in turn, based on historical sales.

Some managers view the scheduling process as haphazardly putting employees' names on a form along with the hours they are to work. They may even add a few names to cover a shift in case one or more people do not show up. However, these managers have little or no chance of making budget or adhering to the labor standard.

Creating a work schedule should only occur after careful planning. First, historical sales figures must be analyzed. Then these historical figures must be translated into a sales projection. Based on the sales projection, the dollars available for labor cost can be determined. Once this is completed, the FICA, Medicare, unemployment insurance benefit costs, and managements' salaries are backed out of the labor cost, leaving the actual number of dollars available to schedule. At this point, a master schedule can be developed, and from that, a crew schedule.

Historical Sales Analysis

Gathering sales history is important because what has occurred in the past is likely to occur in the future. This is particularly true for the foodservice industry. Most operations fall into a pattern of business volume. Historical sales information is simply an account of past sales volumes in a foodservice operation. This historical pattern is valuable in developing sales projections that are used to make up the master schedule. Sales are tracked for different periods: yearly, monthly, weekly, daily, meal period, and hourly. Yearly and monthly data are used for budgeting and income statement purposes. Weekly sales information is used for purchasing and scheduling. Daily, meal period, and hourly data are also used for scheduling, in addition to being used for production planning.

Sales information can come from several sources. Yearly and monthly sales information come from the income statement. Hourly, daily, and weekly figures come from point-of-sale (POS) system printouts. In operations that do not have POS systems, this information comes from tabulating guest checks or periodic cash register readings.

Accurate historical sales information for all these time periods is vitally important. Inaccurate information can cause too many employees to be scheduled, which would increase labor costs and reduce profit. Conversely, inaccurate information may result in fewer employees being scheduled than needed, resulting in poor service, and ultimately, a loss of sales.

Sales Projections

Precise sales projections are paramount to developing a sound master schedule. Sales projections are an estimate of future sales based on historical sales records and other information viewed as relevant by management. In developing sales projections, past sales records are used as a baseline. This baseline is either increased or decreased, based on current, local, and national trends. (See *Exhibit 9d.*)

As projected sales increase, the number of employees will increase, and as projected sales decrease, the number of employees will decrease. Therefore, a master schedule is based on a norm. It is created with the idea that a certain sales level will likely be reached. As sales change from that norm, either up or down, the master

Exhibit 9d

Both local trends, such as increased tourism or convention business, and national trends, such as the economy or unemployment rate, affect sales projections.

schedule should be adjusted accordingly. In some operations, more than one master schedule will be needed.

For example, if a new office park is slated to open across the street from a restaurant, then lunch sales would be projected to show an increase over last year. Conversely, if a manufacturing plant in town is expected to shut down, a restaurant would probably lower its projections, as some residents would have little or no disposable income to spend on eating out.

Adjusting Projections According to Trends

Managers need to examine more than just the previous year's sales information when calculating future sales projections. To make the best estimates for a reasonable master schedule, they also need to consider current trends. While local trends are more important than national ones, the latter should not be overlooked. The economy, unemployment, and other national and international events will all affect a person's desire or ability to eat out.

Forecasting Labor Costs

After determining the anticipated sales, management must determine the **payroll dollars,** which are the number of dollars available for payroll for a scheduling period. Payroll dollars are calculated from anticipated labor costs, which can be complicated to calculate. Fortunately, there is a step-by-step process that managers can follow to forecast these costs for their operations.

Step 1: Determine Total Available Labor Dollars

To determine the total available labor dollars for a period, the operation's standard labor cost percent (discussed earlier in this chapter) is multiplied by the projected sales.

$$\text{Standard labor cost percent} \times \text{Projected sales} = \text{Dollars available for labor}$$

For example, if the standard labor cost percentage for the Tiki Hut is 28 percent, and the projected sales forecast for next week is $17,000, the amount of money available for labor that week is $4,760.

$$.28 \times \$17,000 = \$4,760 \text{ available for labor}$$

Step 2: Subtract Costs of Benefits and Deductions

Now that there is a forecasted amount of money available for labor, the next step is to subtract the cost of benefits and deductions. These amounts must be accounted for and subtracted from the total dollars available for labor.

Suppose the Tiki Hut expects to spend $1,748 on benefits and standard deductions during the upcoming one-week period. The dollars available for payroll would now look like this:

Amount available for labor	−	Benefits and deductions	=	Remaining payroll available
$4,760	−	$1,748	=	$3,012

Step 3: Subtract Fixed Labor Costs

Now that the dollar amount available for scheduling employees has been calculated, the next step is to figure how much of payroll is a fixed cost (management salaries) and how much is variable (hourly employees). This is important for creating a work schedule because, for the most part, only the variable cost employees are listed.

To figure how many dollars are available for scheduling hourly employees, subtract the total of fixed-cost (management) salaries from the payroll dollars available.

Payroll dollars available	−	Fixed-cost salaries	=	Dollars available for variable-cost employees

Assume that management salaries at the Tiki Hut total $1,350 per week. Then the labor dollars available for hourly employees are $1,662.

$$\$3,012 \ - \ \$1,350 \ = \ \$1,662$$

Activity

Calculating Payroll Dollars Available

Liz Fal, a manager for Mary's Café, is forecasting her labor cost for the next week. She has projected sales to be $17,000 for the week. She has established a standard labor percent at 26 percent and knows that management salaries for the week will be $1,350 and benefits and deductions will cost $1,697.

1. How many dollars are available for labor for next week?

2. How many dollars are available for payroll for next week?

3. How many payroll dollars are available for hourly staff for next week?

161

Master Schedules

Once you know the dollars available for labor scheduling, you can begin to create a schedule. Creating a good work schedule for a restaurant is difficult, but not impossible. The right number of people with the right combination of experience and productivity levels must be available to work each shift. Foodservice managers often use a master schedule to simplify the preparation of weekly schedules. A **master schedule** is a template, usually a spreadsheet, showing the number of people needed in each position to run the restaurant or foodservice operation. There are no names listed, simply the positions and the number of employees in those positions. To begin to create the master schedule, the manager must forecast how many servers and other staff will be needed to serve the expected customers.

Forecasting Servers on the Master Schedule

Once the amount that can be spent on hourly employees is known, it must be broken down between the front-of-the-house and back-of-the-house positions. The reason for this is the difference in hourly wages paid to these employees. Servers generally receive tips and are therefore paid less by the restaurant than job classifications that do not receive tips.

You can determine the hourly staff needed by using productivity standards. The most efficient method of scheduling the service staff is by using a labor productivity standard known as covers per server. **Covers per server** are the number of customer meals that a waitstaff member can serve in an hour. Each operation should have a standard figure for covers per server that is based on past customer counts and productivity levels. This standard is then measured against the sales forecast to determine the number of servers to schedule.

At the Tiki Hut, the production standard is twenty covers per server per hour. The forecast for a daily lunch rush (assuming a 4-hour period) is 300 covers. Using this information, 3.75 servers must be scheduled.

300 covers ÷ **4 hours** = **75 covers per hour**

75 covers per hour ÷ **20 covers per server** = **3.75 servers**

The number of servers to schedule is rarely even. The question then becomes: round up or round down? There is no static answer, as it depends on the employees involved. If the staff is relatively new and not fully trained, it would be wise to round up and add another person. On the other hand, if the staff is experienced with a high productivity ratio, it would probably be best to drop a person.

Some people say that a server's tip is solely determined by the customer. Do you agree with this statement? In what ways might the server and other foodservice personnel influence the tip?

Exhibit 9e

Standard Service Schedule for the Tiki Hut

Position	10 a.m.	11 a.m.	12 p.m.	1 p.m.	2 p.m.	Total
Total covers	15	75	80	90	40	**300**
Server A						5 hours
Server B						4 hours
Server C						3 hours
Server D						3 hours
Total hours						**15 hours**

The service schedule should then be further refined, as not all of the guests are going to arrive in an orderly fashion of seventy-five guests per hour. In the example shown in *Exhibit 9e*, during the hour of 12:00–1:00 p.m., a spike of ninety covers is expected, which is ten covers more than the standard for the four servers. During this time period, the waitstaff will be working at a maximum rate with four servers. Consequently, the schedule may call for one server to open and then more servers can be added as the customer count increases over the meal period. Given these patterns, the schedule would look similar to the one shown in *Exhibit 9e*.

Forecasting Other Positions on the Master Schedule

Once the servers are scheduled, the number of hours available for the rest of the positions needs to be determined. How does management know what amount is left to work with? Determining the remaining payroll dollars available is calculated using the following formula:

Payroll dollars available − **Fixed payroll dollars** − **Server payroll dollars** = **Remaining payroll dollars available**

At the Tiki Hut, four servers have been scheduled for the time period of 10:00 a.m. to 2:00 p.m. You can see in *Exhibit 9e* that the total hours for servers for that shift are fifteen. Assuming a rate of $2.13 per hour, the server payroll for the day is $31.95. Assuming the restaurant is open 6 days, the server payroll for the week is $191.70. Look at the remaining payroll dollars available for the other hourly positions at the Tiki Hut:

$3,012 − $1,350 − $192 = $1,470

At this point, the remaining payroll dollars available are divided by the average wage per hour to determine the number of hours available to schedule. Again, each operation should use a standard figure for its average wage per hour. Keep in mind that this standard is an average, and that some employees will make more than this and some will make less.

$$\text{Remaining payroll dollars available} \div \text{Average wage per hour} = \text{Number of hours available to schedule remaining hourly employees}$$

The resulting number gives the manager a good idea of how many hours are left to work with. Assuming the average hourly rate per hour at the Tiki Hut is $7.50, the number of hours remaining available to schedule hourly employees for the week can be determined.

$1,470 ÷ $7.50 = 196 hours

Activity

Forecasting Positions for the Master Schedule

Liz Fal is forecasting positions on the master schedule for Mary's Café on Broadway in Manhattan for next Tuesday. She expects that her staff will serve 300 customers in a five-hour period. Her operation's standard is twenty covers per hour for servers.

1 How many servers will Liz need to schedule? _____

2 If she pays servers $6.75 per hour, how many server payroll dollars will she need for Tuesday? _____

3 If Liz has $277.95 payroll dollars available for hourly staff, how many payroll dollars will be available for positions other than servers? _____

Completing the Master Schedule

At the Tiki Hut, a host/cashier, a busser, a dishwasher, two cooks, and a salad person must be added to the four servers already scheduled to work. The master schedule would then look like the one shown in *Exhibit 9f.*

Based on this master schedule, the total payroll for one day at the Tiki Hut is $276.95. This total includes servers as well as all other hourly (variable-cost) staff. To determine the total variable payroll for the week, assume a 6-day workweek.

$276.95 × 6 days = $1,661.70

Exhibit 9f

Master Schedule for the Tiki Hut

Time	8:00	9:00	10:00	11:00	12:00	1:00	2:00	Total Hours	Rate	Total Payroll
Covers			15	75	80	90	40			
Position										
Server A			✗	✗	✗	✗	✗	5	$ 2.13	$ 10.65
Server B				✗	✗	✗	✗	4	2.13	8.52
Server C				✗	✗	✗		3	2.13	6.39
Server D				✗	✗	✗		3	2.13	6.39
Host/cashier			✗	✗	✗	✗	✗	5	$ 7.50	$ 37.50
Busser				✗	✗	✗	✗	4	6.00	24.00
Dishwasher				✗	✗	✗	✗	4	6.50	26.00
Cook 1	✗	✗	✗	✗	✗	✗		6	10.00	60.00
Cook 2		✗	✗	✗	✗	✗	✗	6	8.00	48.00
Salads	✗	✗	✗	✗	✗	✗		6	8.25	49.50
Total										$276.95

Validating Forecasted Labor Costs

Once the master schedule is written, it needs to be validated to see if it meets the company standard. Managers perform this validation by adding the fixed payroll cost and the variable payroll cost to get total payroll cost. The employer's share of FICA and Medicare and the cost of employee benefits are added to total payroll cost to get the total labor cost.

$$\text{Fixed payroll} + \text{Variable payroll} = \text{Total payroll}$$

$$\text{Total payroll} + \begin{array}{c}\text{FICA/Medicare/}\\\text{unemployment}\\\text{insurance}\\\text{(employer's}\\\text{share only)}\end{array} + \begin{array}{c}\text{Employee}\\\text{benefits}\end{array} = \begin{array}{c}\text{Total}\\\text{forecasted}\\\text{labor cost}\end{array}$$

The total forecasted labor cost is divided by the forecasted sales. The result is the forecasted labor cost percent.

$$\text{Total forecasted labor cost} \div \text{Forecasted sales} = \text{Forecasted labor cost percent}$$

The manager compares the forecasted labor cost percent to the company standard. If all the work has been carefully done to this point, the forecasted labor percent should agree with the company standard. If it does not, then further adjustments must be made.

If the forecast is lower than the standard, then hours need to be added to the schedule. While this may seem counterproductive at first (after all, adding hours will increase costs, which will lower profits), this is not the case. Remember that management determines a standard based on many factors, not the least of which is profit. When considering labor standard, management takes into account producing a quality product and providing quality service. To go under the standard could sacrifice product or service excellence. For this reason, it is just as important to come up to the standard as it is to come down to the standard.

Conversely, if the forecasted labor cost is higher than the standard, then hours need to be cut from the schedule. Adding or cutting hours must be done carefully. If hours are added, they must be added where they will have the most impact on the customer. Where they are cut, they must be cut where they will have the least customer impact.

Think About It...

Have you ever been scheduled to work but really wanted the night off? What would have happened if you did not show up for your shift? What would have been the implications for management, other employees, or even you?

Creating the Crew Schedule

Now that the master schedule has been written, validated, and meets the company standard, it can be used as the foundation for preparing both the management and crew schedules. A **crew schedule** is a chart that shows employees' names and the days and times they are to work. (See *Exhibit 9g.*) Although the target employees are different, there are common considerations for both groups. These include:

- Using all the elements of the master schedule as a source of information for the management and crew schedules

- Communicating well in advance and considering various events and business needs when developing the schedules

- Keeping the schedule as balanced and equitable as possible for all employees

- Building flexibility into the schedules

- Using sales projections to ensure that the right number of employees are scheduled

- Keeping in mind the legal constraints regarding scheduling overtime hours and minors

Exhibit 9g

Crew Schedule for the Tiki Hut, Week of June 20

Name	Position	Monday	Tuesday	Wednesday	Thursday	Friday	Saturday
Brenda	Server	10–3	10–3	10–3	10–3	10–3	10–3
Sung Lee	Server	11–3	11–3	11–3	11–3	11–3	11–3
James	Server	11–2	11–2	11–2	11–2	11–2	11–2
Tony	Server	11–2	11–2	11–2	11–2	11–2	11–2
Rubin	Host/ Cashier	10–3	10–3	10–3	10–3	10–3	10–3
Wendy	Busser	11–3	11–3	11–3	11–3	11–3	11–3
Mike	Dishwasher	11–3	11–3	11–3	11–3	11–3	11–3
Carlo	Cook 1	8–2	8–2	8–2	8–2	8–2	8–2
Judy	Cook 2	9–3	9–3	9–3	9–3	8–2	8–2
Tonya	Salads	8–2	8–2	8–2	8–2	8–2	8–2

Controlling Labor Costs

The primary control for managing labor cost is the schedule. It must be accurate. If it is incorrect, all other controls become less effective. The most difficult part of proper scheduling is forecasting sales. Sales dictate how much staff to schedule for a particular period. However, factors that are unknown when the schedule is written can undermine even the most careful planning. An unforeseen winter storm can virtually close down a neighborhood restaurant but stretch an interstate highway restaurant to beyond its capacity. A sudden thunderstorm will keep people inside, but a power outage caused by the storm will bring them out of their houses to get something to eat. Factors other than weather, such as earthquakes, crime sprees, and a national or international event on television will also affect people's behavior. In addition, there is sometimes no apparent reason for a spike or lag in sales.

The astute manager will make adjustments to the schedule to accommodate these circumstances. Consider the fact that unneeded payroll adds up quickly and cannot be made up. For example, if the standard payroll percentage is 30 percent and sales drop $500 below budget for a particular night, then payroll is $150 over budget ($500 × .30 = $150). If sales are at budget the next night, management cannot take $150 off payroll, since that would result in poor service. Therefore the $150 is "lost." If, however, there is a trend of sales being below budget, then management should take immediate action and cut the schedule accordingly.

Care must be taken when adjusting the schedule. Employees are dependent on the income provided by working their posted hours, and they also plan activities outside of work based on the posted schedule. By frequently changing the schedule, the manager risks alienating some staff members and contributing to employee turnover. There is little margin for error when planning a schedule so that it meets the labor cost standard, and yet allows for the appropriate number of staff to properly take care of customers.

Keeping Track of Time

Another control in maintaining labor cost is tracking the time that employees work. There are three methods to do this—time sheet, timecard, and time-clock software.

- **Time sheet**—Post a chart with all of the employees' names near the schedule. When the employee comes to work, he or she marks the time of arrival and initials the chart. When the employee leaves at the end of the shift, he or she marks the time of departure and initials the chart.

- **Timecard**—Each employee has a timecard placed in a timecard rack. When the employee reports to work, he or she inserts the timecard into a time clock. When the employee leaves at the end of the shift, he or she does the same thing and places the timecard back in the rack. In this way, the employee's arrival and departure times are recorded on the timecard.

- **Electronic method**—This includes electronic time clocks, POS (point-of-sale) systems, and personal computers with time-clock software. (See *Exhibit 9h*.) The employee is assigned a password and when arriving at work, he or she inputs the password. The software records the time. When the employee leaves at the end of the shift, he or she inputs the password. Many of these electronic systems have payroll software that will calculate the total hours worked during a payroll period, along with federal and state withholding, FICA, and other deductions like health insurance, and will then calculate the employee's paycheck. In some chain operations, the system is tied into the accounting department in the home office.

Regardless of which system is used, it is imperative that a manager or bookkeeper review the time recorded by the employee and compare it to the schedule. Some employees have a habit of coming to work before their shift, clocking in, and then spending some time visiting with other employees before actually beginning to work. The same thing can happen at the end of an employee's shift. It only takes a few of these occurrences to put labor cost out of line.

Exhibit 9h

POS systems can simplify the collection of payroll data.

If you were a hospitality and restaurant consultant, what might you say to a new restaurant entrepreneur who was planning to open a restaurant in an area where competition for labor is fierce? What would be some of the key strategies regarding labor cost controls that you would share with this person?

There are a few exceptions of employees working outside of the schedule. In most states, an employee must be paid for attending an employee meeting. They should clock in and out for these meetings. In some states, when an employer requires that employees wear uniforms, they must allow the employee to change clothes on company time. In this case, a reasonable amount of time should be allocated for the employee to change. While under these circumstances, the employee is working off the schedule; under no circumstances should employees be allowed to work off the clock. If employees are working, they should be clocked in and paid. Not only is this the ethical way to treat employees, it is also necessary for liability insurance.

Overtime

Nothing can make a labor cost go over budget quicker than overtime. Federal law, as well as the laws of most states, requires that nonmanagement employees working **overtime**—any hours worked over forty hours in a workweek—be compensated for overtime hours at a rate of at least one and one-half times the employee's regular rate of pay. At that rate, it does not take long to use available payroll dollars. Overtime should never be scheduled or planned. Only in an extreme circumstance should management authorize an employee to work overtime.

Other Factors that Affect Labor Cost Directly

While scheduling has a direct effect on labor cost on a day-to-day basis, there are other factors that also significantly influence labor cost. Employee turnover, employee benefits, and labor contracts all affect labor cost directly, while quality and productivity standards affect it indirectly. Scheduling is the prevalent labor cost control, but other factors also contribute to effective labor cost control.

Employee Turnover

Employee turnover—the number of employees hired to fill one position in a year's time—is a factor that directly impacts labor cost. Unfortunately, it is a widespread problem in the restaurant and foodservice industry. While some turnover is normal, excessive turnover is a major problem. Some restaurant chains have turnover rates of 300 percent. This means that for every position the restaurant has, three people have been hired during the year to fill that position.

To calculate the turnover rate, count the number of employees hired during the year and divide by the average number of employees needed. Multiply the result by 100 to convert the decimal into a percent. The result is the turnover rate percent.

$$\text{Persons hired per year} \div \text{Average number of employees} = \text{Turnover}$$

$$\text{Turnover} \times 100 = \text{Turnover rate percent}$$

For example, if a restaurant needed 50 employees to operate, and over a year it hired 150 people, its turnover rate would be 300 percent.

$$\text{150 persons hired} \div \text{50 employees needed} = 3$$

$$3 \times 100 = 300\%$$

Not all restaurants have a high turnover rate. Those that can control turnover have a better chance of making payroll budget because turnover is very costly. Consider these expenses associated with turnover:

- Lost management time for interviewing, holding orientation meetings, and training new employees
- Labor cost of employee that the new hire "shadows"
- Unproductive time of the new employee on the payroll during training
- Cost of want ads, online help-wanted advertisements, temp agencies, and employment agencies
- Accounting costs associated with employees who have left the company and new hires

While few companies track the exact cost of employee turnover, it can be expensive. Taking a conservative figure of $150 per hire, if a restaurant hires 25 new employees during the year, the cost is $3,750. If, as in the example above, 150 employees are hired during the year, the cost of the new hires is $22,500 (150 × $150). The cost for hiring comes directly out of profit.

Direct expenses not withstanding, there are indirect costs of turnover to the restaurant as well. Two of the most prevalent indirect costs are loss of productivity and customer dissatisfaction due to the inefficiencies and mistakes of a new hire.

It should be obvious that reducing employee turnover will not only improve the bottom line, but will also result in a smoother running operation ultimately resulting in customer satisfaction. To reduce employee turnover, a manager should examine why employees leave in the first place. Some employees depart for other restaurant or foodservice operations while some leave the industry altogether. Studies have shown that there are several reasons for this departure. *Exhibit 9i* lists many of these reasons along with possible ways that management can relieve these situations. While there are other causes of turnover, *Exhibit 9i* lists the most prevalent ones.

Exhibit 9i

Reasons for Turnover

Reasons for Turnover	Remedy or Possible Solution
Stress	■ Have the proper number of well-trained staff in place. This provides a calm and amiable atmosphere where everyone works together as a team to get the job done.
	■ Use "what if" questions during the interview process to eliminate individuals who cannot deal with stressful situations that are common to the industry.
Income	■ Make sure that employees are being paid a competitive wage.
	■ Consider adding employee benefits to the compensation package.
Working conditions	■ Heat and humidity can be taken out of kitchens with a good ventilation system.
■ Hot and humid kitchens	
■ Crowded dining rooms	■ Consider removing some tables so that proper traffic patterns can develop.
■ Slippery floors	
■ Crowded traffic patterns	■ Ensure that spills are cleaned up immediately.
	■ Move equipment to reduce steps and use better-designed facilities.
Supervision	■ Problems arise when rules, policies, and procedures are not applied uniformly.
	■ Ensure that all management understands the necessity of administering rules and policies fairly and equitably.

Activity

Calculating Turnover Rate Percentage

1 Universe Café needs 34 employees to operate, and over the course of a year it hires 87 people. What is the turnover rate?

2 Turquoise Bar and Grill needs 56 employees to operate, and over the course of a year it hires 126 people. What is the turnover rate?

3 Connor's Steakhouse needs 84 employees to operate, and over the course of a year it hires 56 people. What is the turnover rate?

Think About It...

Which employee benefits are most desirable to you? Why?

Employee Benefits

The employee benefits that a restaurant or foodservice organization offer also affect its labor cost. Some organizations offer few, if any benefits. Others offer many benefits to its employees, some of which include:

- Paid holidays
- Paid vacation
- Health insurance
- Dental insurance
- Employee assistance program
- Life insurance
- Substance abuse assistance
- Day care
- Transportation assistance
- Fitness center

Employee benefits typically are linked to how competitive the labor market is. In a small town, an independent restaurant may give some paid holidays and a paid vacation as its package, while a chain restaurant in a large city that is heavily unionized may offer a significant employee benefit package. Because of this range, the cost varies widely from restaurant to restaurant. For example, a modest health insurance package alone may cost $5,000 yearly per employee or $14,000 for an employee and his or her family, and the cost is increasing annually at an alarming rate. Some companies differentiate between salaried and hourly employees, giving salaried employees more benefits than hourly employees, due to the competitive nature of finding talented managers.

Employee benefits, while expensive, are necessary in many cases to attract and retain good staff members. In terms of employee turnover, a company with a good employee benefit program has a definite advantage.

Labor Contracts

An organized labor contract can have a huge impact on a restaurant's labor cost. Unions in the hospitality industry are limited primarily to large metropolitan areas such as New York, Chicago, and Los Angeles, as well as entertainment destinations such as Las Vegas. A **labor contract** is an agreement between management and a union that represents the employees and deals with wages, employee benefits, hours, and working conditions.

In an operation with a labor contract, the wages, employee benefits, and working conditions are all negotiated. The union, which represents the employees, and a member of management conduct the negotiations. However, it is important for the negotiations to be settled in a way that is acceptable to management and can keep labor costs within their controls.

For the most part, restaurants that are under a labor contract will have a higher labor cost. This higher cost is due to higher wages being paid and more employee benefits provided in union operations than in nonunion operations. In addition to wages and benefits, production output, layoff procedures, and disciplinary actions might also need to be negotiated. These actions also increase labor costs since management cannot get higher productivity out of employees and cannot lay employees off during a downturn in sales.

Factors That Affect Labor Cost Indirectly

In addition to the issues that affect labor cost directly, there are several indirect factors. While these factors do not have a direct impact on labor cost, they warrant management's attention since they can cause an operation's labor cost to get out of line. These factors are quality and productivity standards. A **quality standard** is a level of excellence used to measure customer satisfaction, while a **productivity standard** is a level set by management to measure the amount of work performed by an employee. The key word here is "standard." Before management can measure an employee's effectiveness, they must develop standards. Some of the standards may include:

- **Job description**—Every position in the restaurant should have a **job description,** which is a statement that details an employee's duties and the standard to which he or she is expected to perform those duties. A job description should include company quality and productivity standards. See *Exhibit 9j* for a list of the standards that might be part of a server's job description.

- **Menu**—Lists quality standards, such as a USDA grade and descriptive terminology like "crisp" or "green." It also lists quantity standards such as twelve-ounce, extra-large portion, or petite portion.

- **Production chart**—Has quantity standards regarding how much to prepare.

- **Standardized recipe**—Specifies the quality level of a product as well as the number of portions.

These examples are among the most widely used of the forms, charts, and documents that provide employees with management's performance standards. Once standards are developed, it is up to management to ensure that they are followed.

Quality Standards

Quality standards are particularly important since they not only affect labor cost but also affect the product that the customer receives. The primary reason for establishing quality standards is to have a measure in place to assure that customers receive the products they pay for. However, in an indirect way, quality standards also affect labor cost.

If an employee does not prepare a product that meets standard, it must be redone. This costs money, not only in terms of wasted product that increases food cost, but also in terms of productivity that increases labor cost. To track product in the back of the house that does not meet standard, a waste report is used. As explained in Chapter 7, the waste report gives management a tool to track any potential problems with food preparation standards.

To track quality standards in the front of the house, many operations use a **return chart** as seen in *Exhibit 9k*. This chart is filled out to explain why a customer returned an item to the kitchen.

Since the waste report and return chart are similar, many operations combine them into one. Whichever method an operation uses, management must review the charts on a daily basis and take action to correct the problems, since they will have an effect on the profitability of the operation.

Exhibit 9k

Sample Return Chart

RETURN CHART

DATE: Dec. 06

FILLED OUT BY: *M.L.*

Item	Server	Check No.	Reason returned	Initial
Chicken fried steak	Bill	X0335	Not what customer ordered	3 W
Chilled fruit plate	Carlos	X4783	Hair on plate	C
Reuben	Ann	Y2331	Plate dropped	A.L.
Rib eye steak	LaToya	A3951	Overcooked	L.J.
Tomato rice soup	Margie	B5789	Too salty	M.B.
French fries	Carlos	X4791	Cold	C
Sushi platter	LaToya	A3962	Smelled fishy	L.J.

Productivity Standards

Productivity is measured in three ways:

- Sales per person-hour

- Covers per person-hour

- Sales per cover

You will notice that two of these measures of productivity use person-hour as a basis for comparison. **Person-hours,** also called labor hours, are the total hours worked by hourly (variable-cost) employees for a given period of time. To calculate person-hours, multiply the number of employees by the hours they worked. For example, if 3 people each worked the cook's line yesterday for 5 hours, then the cook's line used 15 person-hours.

3 people × 5 hours = 15 person-hours

Typically, person-hours are calculated only for hourly staff, since they are paid for the actual number of hours they work. Salaried employees normally do not work a fixed number of hours, but rather put in the hours necessary to get the job done.

Sales Per Person-Hour

By using person-hours as the basis for comparison, management can calculate sales per person-hour. Sales per person-hour gives an indication of how productive staff is. Sales per person-hour can be calculated for any sales period—hour, meal, day, week, month, or year. To figure sales per person-hour, divide sales for the period by the number of person-hours worked during that period. For example, to measure the productivity of the cook's line, assume that sales for the lunch shift were $1,000 and the line used 15 person-hours, then the sales per person-hour was $66.67.

Sales ÷ Number of person-hours = Sales per person-hour

$1,000 ÷ 15 = $66.67

Management can calculate sales per person-hour for the cook's line during other lunch shifts in a week to compare the productivity of different teams on the cook's line. Since the line function is normally a team effort, management can see over time that some combinations of people are more productive than other combinations and can schedule accordingly. However, a word of caution is needed when comparing sales per person-hour. Only compare shifts with like shifts; that is, compare breakfast shifts with breakfast shifts, lunch with lunch, and so on. The reason for this is that check averages vary greatly from breakfast to lunch to dinner. To compare sales per person-hour at breakfast to sales per person-hour at dinner would be meaningless.

Comparison of sales per person-hour between periods of time is valuable information. However, the real power of the comparison occurs when the current sales per person-hour is compared to the standard that management has set for each department in the operation. Results should always be compared to the standard. If a department is not measuring up to standard, the reason should be investigated and corrective action taken to bring the results back into line.

How management interprets and uses sales per person-hour depends on the department being analyzed. For example, sales per person-hour is interpreted differently for servers than for line cooks. Since sales per person-hour can be used to measure a server's ability to sell, management should set a standard for server sales per person-hour. Waitstaff who do not measure up to the standard should be given additional training to increase their sales ability.

Covers Per Person–Hour

Covers per person-hour is a different way to look at productivity and is figured in the same way as sales per person-hour. To figure covers per person-hour, divide the number of covers sold by the number of person-hours.

Covers ÷ Person-hours = Covers per person-hour

For example, management wants to track the productivity of the dishwashing operation. Two dishwashers were on hand for a lunch shift of 225 covers. One dishwasher worked 5 hours and one worked 4 hours, for a total of 9 person-hours. The covers per person-hour for the dishwashing crew would then be figured as follows:

225 covers ÷ 9 person-hours = 25 covers per person-hour

Similar periods must be compared to similar periods. For example, it would not be fair to compare the covers per person-hour of a breakfast shift with the covers per person-hour for a dinner shift. For dishwashers, the dinner shift would have more china, glassware, and flatware to wash than the breakfast shift. Likewise, when reviewing server productivity, keep in mind that customers typically take more time to eat dinner than they do to eat breakfast. Consequently, fewer covers per person-hour will be served at dinner than at breakfast.

As with sales per person-hour, management must establish standards for each position and each shift and compare actual covers per person-hour against the appropriate standard. Another use of covers

Activity

Labor Costs and Personnel Issues

Pat Consoro is the Operations Manager for an upscale restaurant in Santa Fe, New Mexico. Both locals and frequent tourists come to the restaurant to savor some of the best southwestern cuisine that the city has to offer. Pat needs an additional host or hostess because of the increasing popularity of the restaurant. Pat is interviewing Terry, an excellent candidate who has seven years experience and is currently working at another local restaurant, which is a competitor. Normally, Pat starts a hostess at $13.50 per hour. However, Terry has indicated that in her present position, her hourly rate is $15.00. This is a higher rate than any of the other hostesses Pat currently has, except for Suzanne, who has been on staff for ten years. Terry has indicated that she would not leave her current position for a position with a lower rate.

Work in small groups to answer the following questions. Share your group's responses with the entire class.

1 Should Pat hire Terry at a rate higher than most of the current staff? Why or why not?

_____

_____

_____

_____

2 If you indicated "no," what would you say to Terry?

_____

_____

_____

_____

3 If you indicated "yes," what would you say to your current hostess staff?

_____

_____

_____

_____

4 What factors would you need to consider in your decision-making process?

_____

_____

_____

_____

per person-hour is for scheduling staff. By anticipating the total number of covers for a particular meal period, management can determine the number of servers to schedule.

Sales Per Cover

A third productivity measure that is especially useful for measuring server productivity is sales per cover. When analyzed together, sales per cover and covers per person-hour will indicate who the best servers are in terms of productivity (table turnover) and sales ability (high average check). Sales per cover measures the sales ability of a server—the higher the sales per cover dollar amount, the more that server is selling, on average, to each customer. To figure sales per cover, divide the total sales for the server by the number of covers sold by the server.

Total sales per server ÷ **Covers sold by server** = **Sales per cover**

Assume that LaToya had sales of $900 yesterday evening and served 55 covers.

$900 ÷ 55 covers = $16.36 per cover

Contrast this to Hunter, who had $1,050 in sales for the same meal period and served 70 covers.

$1,050 ÷ 70 covers = $15.00 per cover

Even though Hunter had a higher sales total and served more covers, his sales per cover was lower than LaToya's.

As with other measures of productivity, sales per cover must be analyzed over a period of time, as there are too many factors that can distort the figures for one shift. In addition, when comparing one server's performance to another server's performance, management must compare performance for the same time period.

However, management must be careful when trying to increase sales per cover that service quality is not negatively impacted.

Think About It...

What factors might have a positive impact on sales per cover?

Summary

This chapter introduced the elements that help management control labor cost. Labor cost includes, in addition to payroll cost, such costs as the employer's contribution to FICA and Medicare, workers' compensation insurance, and employee benefits. Although total labor cost might be a large number, management is most concerned about the relationship between labor cost and sales. By looking at labor cost as a percentage, the relationship between labor cost and sales is taken into account. With labor being one of the highest costs for which management is responsible, it is imperative that management uses every tool available to control this cost.

One control management uses to keep labor cost in control is the budget. Having a budget helps managers plan the financial activities related to their daily operations. For an operation to achieve its budgeted profit, the sales projections listed in its budget must be met. Additionally, the operation's costs must be held to their standards. Accurate historical sales information and projected sales are vitally important to an accurate budget. Budget accuracy is important because the budget is the foundation on which management builds the master schedule.

The primary control for managing labor cost is the schedule. Once you know the dollars available for labor scheduling, you can begin to create a schedule. The right number of people with the right combination of experience and productivity levels must be available to work each shift. If too many people are scheduled, labor costs increase. Conversely, if too few people are scheduled, service may be poor and result in a loss of sales. Restaurant and foodservice managers often use a master schedule to simplify the preparation of weekly schedules. There is little margin for error when planning a schedule so that it meets the labor cost standard and still allows for the appropriate number of staff to provide good service.

While scheduling has a direct effect on labor cost on a day-to-day basis, there are other factors that directly influence it, including employee turnover, employee benefits, and labor contracts. Quality and productivity standards affect labor cost indirectly. Management can use sales per person-hour, covers per person-hour, and sales per cover to monitor productivity and to spot problems before they cause an increase in labor cost.

Review Your Learning

1 The contribution rate for FICA is

   A. 6.2 percent paid by the employee.

   B. 6.2 percent paid by the employer.

   C. Both A and B

   D. Neither A nor B

2 For a restaurant to make its annual budget projection

   A. the sales budget must be met.

   B. the cost lines must be held to their budgeted amount.

   C. Both A and B

   D. Neither A nor B

3 Employee benefits

   A. are additional costs to monitor.

   B. are necessary to attract good employees.

   C. can be given to management and not to hourly employees.

   D. A, B, and C

Monthly data for **4** through **8**:

Sales: $80,000
Standard labor cost percent: 28 percent
Fixed cost payroll: $8,000
Employee benefit cost: $1,500
Server payroll dollars: $840
Average hourly wage without servers: $7.15

4 The total dollars available for labor cost are

   A. $19,740.

   B. $20,160.

   C. $22,400.

   D. Cannot be determined from data given

5 The FICA and Medicare amount paid by the employer is

   A. $1,389.

   B. $1,725.

   C. $4,960.

   D. Cannot be determined from data given

6 The total dollars available for payroll are

   A. $11,175.

   B. $16,935.

   C. $19,175.

   D. Cannot be determined from data given

7 The variable dollars available for scheduling are

   A. $11,175.

   B. $12,900.

   C. $19,175.

   D. Cannot be determined from data given

8 The estimated number of hours that can be scheduled for this month excluding servers is

   A. 1,445.

   B. 1,567.

   C. 2,146.

   D. 2,445.

9 If a restaurant needs 12 employees to operate and hires 50 employees during the year, its turnover rate is

   A. 24 percent.

   B. 41.7 percent.

   C. 240 percent.

   D. 417 percent.

10 **Turnover is most frequently caused by**

A. on-the-job stress.

B. poor working conditions.

C. low wages.

D. All of the above

11 **Labor cost includes**

A. payroll.

B. FICA and Medicare.

C. employee benefits.

D. A, B, and C

12 **Labor cost is controlled to a**

A. standard dollar amount.

B. standard percent.

C. Both A and B

D. Neither A nor B

13 **Budgets are based on**

A. historical sales and costs.

B. projected sales and costs.

C. Both A and B

D. Neither A nor B

14 **The most efficient way to determine the number of servers to schedule is**

A. covers per person-hour.

B. average wage per hour.

C. sales per cover.

D. Both A and B

15 **The number of persons needed to fill a shift is dependent on**

A. the menu, type of service, and complexity of production.

B. the style of a restaurant, its location, and its price point.

C. Both A and B

D. Neither A nor B

16 **Labor contracts**

A. increase the average hourly rate.

B. normally have greater employee benefits for employees.

C. affect production output.

D. A, B, and C

Notes

Appendix

Math skills are extremely important in restaurant and foodservice operations. Managers are expected to have a basic understanding of math and know how to apply mathematical principles to business situations. Math skills are also essential in the professional kitchen. Chefs and managers need to know how to determine recipe yields, convert recipes from customary to metric measure, and change the yields of recipes.

This appendix is a review of some basic math concepts.

Mathematical Operations

As you have learned in previous math classes, there are several operations performed on numbers, and each corresponds to a familiar symbol. Numbers can be added ($10 + 2 = 12$), subtracted ($10 - 2 = 8$), multiplied ($10 \times 2 = 20$), and divided ($10 \div 2 = 5$). They can also be expressed as fractions, which is the same as dividing them ($\frac{10}{2} = 10 \div 2 = 5$).

These four basic math functions are the basis upon which all other mathematical functions are performed. Knowing all four functions well will help you as you continue to learn about business math.

Addition

Numbers are added by lining them up in columns and then assigning each column of digits a value of 1, 10, 100, 1,000, and so on, beginning with the right-most column. In the number 372, for example, 2 is in the *ones* column, 7 is in the *tens* column, and 3 is in the *hundreds* column.

When adding a column, if the sum of a column contains two digits, then the right digit is written below the sum line, and the left digit is added to the next column as you move from right to left.

$$
\begin{array}{r}
1 \\
24 \\
+\,17 \\
\hline
41
\end{array}
$$

Subtraction

When subtracting large numbers, a technique known as borrowing is often used. If a digit in one column is too large to be subtracted from the digit above it, then 10 is borrowed from the column immediately to the left.

$$
\begin{array}{r}
7\,1 \\
\cancel{8}\cancel{2} \\
-\,17 \\
\hline
65
\end{array}
$$

To check your work on a subtraction problem, simply add the answer to the subtracted number. The result should be the first number.

$$
\begin{array}{rl}
1 & \\
65 & \text{(answer)} \\
+\,17 & \text{(subtracted number)} \\
\hline
82 &
\end{array}
$$

Multiplication

To multiply large numbers, the digit in the ones column of the second number is first multiplied by the digits above it, going from right to left.

For example, to solve 32 × 4:

■ Multiply 4 by 2; result is 8.

$$
\begin{array}{r}
3\mathbf{2} \\
\times\,4 \\
\hline
\mathbf{8}
\end{array}
$$

■ Multiply 4 by 3; result is 12.

$$
\begin{array}{r}
\mathbf{3}2 \\
\times\,4 \\
\hline
1\mathbf{28}
\end{array}
$$

The final result is 128.

Exhibit A1 will help you review multiplication for the numbers 1 through 12.

Exhibit A1

Multiplication Table

	1	2	3	4	5	6	7	8	9	10	11	12
1	1	2	3	4	5	6	7	8	9	10	11	12
2	2	4	6	8	10	12	14	16	18	20	22	24
3	3	6	9	12	15	18	21	24	27	30	33	36
4	4	8	12	16	20	24	28	32	36	40	44	48
5	5	10	15	20	25	30	35	40	45	50	55	60
6	6	12	18	24	30	36	42	48	54	60	66	72
7	7	14	21	28	35	42	49	56	63	70	77	84
8	8	16	24	32	40	48	56	64	72	80	88	96
9	9	18	27	36	45	54	63	72	81	90	99	108
10	10	20	30	40	50	60	70	80	90	100	110	120
11	11	22	33	44	55	66	77	88	99	110	121	132
12	12	24	36	48	60	72	84	96	108	120	132	144

Division

Larger numbers are divided using a combination of division and subtraction. The dividend is placed inside the long division sign, and the divisor is placed outside. For example, in the problem 728 ÷ 14, 728 is the dividend, and 14 is the divisor.

To solve 728 ÷ 14:

1 Divide 14 into 72; result is 5.
$14 \times 5 = 70$
Subtract from 72.

$$
\begin{array}{r}
5 \\
14\overline{)72}8 \\
-70 \\
\hline
2
\end{array}
$$

2 Bring down 8.
Divide 14 into 28; result is 2.
$14 \times 2 = 28$
Subtract from 28.

$$
\begin{array}{r}
52 \\
14\overline{)72}8 \\
-70 \\
\hline
28 \\
-28 \\
\hline
0
\end{array}
$$

The final result is 52.

Fractions, Decimals, and Percentages

Fractions

In adding and subtracting fractions, the denominators, the lower portion of the fraction must be the same (for example $\frac{1}{3} + \frac{1}{3} = \frac{2}{3}$). When the denominators are the same, the numerators, the upper portion of a fraction, are added and subtracted the same way as whole numbers.

If the denominators to be added or subtracted are different from each other, then you must first determine the lowest common denominator, which is the smallest whole number that is evenly divided by each denominator. The next step is to multiply each numerator by the number that its corresponding denominator was multiplied by in order to arrive at the lowest common denominator.

For example, in the next problem, both the numerator and the denominator in $\frac{2}{3}$ are multiplied by 4, giving us the new, equivalent fraction $\frac{8}{12}$.

$$\frac{2}{3} + \frac{3}{4} =$$
$$\frac{8}{12} + \frac{9}{12} = \frac{17}{12}$$
$$\frac{17}{12} = 1\frac{5}{12}$$

Exhibit A2

Common Fractions and their Decimal Equivalents

$\frac{1}{8}$ = 0.125	$\frac{3}{8}$ = 0.375	$\frac{2}{3}$ = 0.6667
$\frac{1}{6}$ = 0.1667	$\frac{1}{2}$ = 0.50	$\frac{3}{4}$ = 0.75
$\frac{1}{4}$ = 0.25	$\frac{5}{8}$ = 0.625	$\frac{7}{8}$ = 0.875

Decimals

Fractions are often expressed as decimals. (See *Exhibit A2.*) All decimals are based on one-tenth, one-hundredth, one-thousandth, etc. For example, 1.4 is 1 and 4-tenths, and 6.21 is 6 and 21-hundredths.

Decimals are added, subtracted, multiplied, and divided just like non-decimal numbers. When adding or subtracting decimals, the key is to line up the decimal points.

$$\begin{array}{r} 8.46 \\ +\,4.23 \\ \hline 12.69 \end{array} \qquad \begin{array}{r} 8.46 \\ -\,4.23 \\ \hline 4.23 \end{array}$$

When multiplying decimals, you must determine where to place the decimal point once you've calculated your final total answer. To do this, count the total number of digits to the right of all decimal points in the numbers that you are multiplying and then place the decimal point in your final answer by counting that many places from the right. For example, there are a total of four digits to the right of the decimal points in 8.46 and 4.23. Therefore, the decimal point goes four places from the right in the answer, 35.7858.

$$\begin{array}{r} 8.46 \\ \times\,4.23 \\ \hline 2538 \\ 16920 \\ 338400 \\ \hline 35.7858 \end{array}$$

When dividing decimals, if the divisor is not a whole number, move the decimal point to the right to make the divisor a whole number. Also move the decimal point in the dividend the same number of places to the right. Divide as usual. In the answer, simply bring the decimal point up directly above the long division sign.

Think About It...

The sports store at the mall is having a 25% discount sale on name brand T-shirts. If the T-shirts usually sell for $15.00, what will the price be during the sale?

$$4.23 \overline{)8.46} = 2$$

When a calculator or computer is used, numbers will often have more digits to the right of the decimal point than are practical or useful. In these cases, numbers are rounded to the nearest tenth, hundredth, or thousandth. Numbers are sometimes rounded to the nearest whole number in order to eliminate the decimal point.

In rounding, if the next digit to the right is less than 5, then the number is usually rounded down (5.12 is rounded to 5.1). If the number to the right is 5 or above, then the number is rounded up (5.19 is rounded to 5.2). The number 5.192635 can be rounded to the nearest thousandth (5.193), hundredth (5.19), tenth (5.2), or whole number (5).

Percentages

One of the first mathematical operations you will come in contact with is percentages. Restaurant and foodservice managers and employees often express numbers as percentages, or parts per 100. If you are working with a fraction that you want to express as a percentage, the first step is to convert the fraction into a decimal. For example, to express $\frac{1}{2}$ as a decimal, the numerator (1) is divided by the denominator (2) for an answer of 0.5. Add a zero (0) in the hundredths place (0.50), and the two digits to the right of the decimal point are expressed as 50 percent, or 50%.

To determine a certain percentage of a given number, it is first expressed as a decimal and then multiplied. For instance, to find 20% of 60, multiply 60 by 0.20.

$$\begin{array}{r} 60 \\ \times 0.20 \\ \hline 00 \\ 1200 \\ \hline 1200 \end{array}$$

Then, place the decimal point as required, so that 1200 becomes 12.00. Thus, 20% of 60 is 12.

You can also determine the percentage of one number to another number. For instance, if 60 customers out of a total of 300 are ordering the house special, the percentage of customers ordering the special is found by dividing the portion (60) by the total (300).

$$\frac{60}{300} = 0.20 = 20\%$$

This equation shows that 60 customers out of the total 300 customers equals 0.20 or 20%. In other words, 20% of the customers are ordering the special.

Review Your Learning

1 A restaurant operator budgets 4% of her total $856,000 budget for marketing. What is her marketing budget? _____

2 In the number 3,897, the 9 occupies which of the following columns?

A. Ones   B. Tens   C. Hundreds   D. Thousands

3 Of 4,500 customers last month, 710 ordered items from the lighter menu selections. What percentage is this? _____

4 A vendor's invoice for purchases is shown below. Calculate the amounts for each item on the invoice, the delivery charge, and the invoice total.

10 cases lettuce	at $35.76/case	$
12 cases tomatoes	at $25.00/case	$
6 cases radishes	at $14.28/case	$
4 cases strawberries	at $47.84/case	$
	Subtotal	$
Next-day delivery charge 7% of order subtotal		$
	Invoice total	$

5 After tabulating the results of a survey sent to frequent customers, an operation determines the following information about how customers rate the establishment's service:

Number of customers	Rating
200	Excellent
250	Very good
330	Good
200	Fair
20	Poor

What percentage of customers rated the operation's service as very good or better?

_____

Notes

Field Project

Cost Control throughout the Flow of Food

This field practicum will provide you with an opportunity to learn from practitioners in the restaurant and foodservice industry and find out how the concepts that have been covered in this guide are used in actual practice. This practicum is designed to give you an in-depth look at how costs must be controlled throughout the many processes an operation must perform.

Assignment

To begin, you must obtain a menu either from the place you work or from a local restaurant. Be sure to get the manager's permission to take a menu.

Part One

List all the menu items that indicate a specific portion size, e.g., six-ounce filet mignon. Create a table with this information, noting if an item is preportioned or portioned when it is plated. (You may have to talk with the manager about this if the menu does not make the distinction clear.)

Part Two

After you complete the table, select three menu items and trace how costs are controlled for each item as it passes through the various stages of the restaurant. Develop a set of questions for each stage that you can ask the restaurant manager or another restaurant staff member. Some sample questions are given below:

1 Purchasing and Receiving

☐ What is the as purchased price of the main ingredients in this menu item?

☐ What is the yield percentage of the main ingredients in this menu item?

☐ What is the EP cost?

☐ What is the EP percentage?

☐ How often do these items need to be purchased?

2 Storing and Issuing

☐ How are the items stored?

☐ What stock rotation method is used?

☐ How is spoilage prevented?

3 Production

☐ How many portions are prepared each day?

☐ Is there a standardized recipe for each menu item?

☐ How are wasted foods tracked?

☐ How is each menu item portioned?

continued on next page

Cost Control Throughout the Flow of Food *continued from previous page*

4 Service and Sales

☐ How was the selling price determined?

☐ What market forces affect the selling price for each menu item?

☐ How are sales tracked?

☐ What methods of payment are accepted?

☐ How is scheduling done?

☐ How does management forecast labor costs?

☐ What is the employee turnover rate?

Part Three

Write a three to five page paper that summarizes your findings. Your report should start with the purchasing process and then move onto production and service. Include in your report how costs are being controlled in this restaurant. Also spend some time predicting what would happen if the costs were not controlled on these items at any point during the flow through the operation.

Index

M

management, 3–5, 7–10, 24, 30, 36, 47, 48, 50, 52–54, 62, 63, 71–72, 74–76, 90. 92, 94, 96, 97, 99, 102, 104, 111–13, 122, 132, 135, 136, 139, 141, 142, 144, 145, 154–160, 163, 166, 170, 172–76, 178

manager, 2–5, 7, 9, 13, 31, 33, 37, 47, 50, 52, 62, 63, 67, 68, 75, 81, 82, 84, 89, 90, 93–95, 97, 102, 105, 115, 116, 134, 135, 156–158, 160, 162, 164–67, 172

market, 49, 50

external market factors, 49

market quotation sheet, 67

markup, 43, 44–47, 49, 50, 112

markup differentiation, 49

Meat Buyers Guide, 64

meat yield test (*see* butcher test)

Medicare, 11, 154, 155, 158, 165

menu, 29, 46, 50, 52–54, 62, 75, 77, 131, 173

cycle menu, 113

daily menu, 113

static menu, 113

menu engineering, 50

menu item, 29, 30, 33, 36, 43–50, 54, 63, 75, 102, 103, 113, 115, 131, 132, 174

menu price, 24, 30, 33, 36, 43–47, 48, 50, 51, 54, 132

calculation of,

factor method, 45

markup on cost method, 45–46

Texas Restaurant Association (TRA) markup method, 43, 44–45, 46

menu product mix, 49–51, 53, 55

spreadsheet, 50–51

minimum wage, 139

monitoring, 11

mortgage, 5

N

nonperishable goods, 73–75, 103

North American Meat Processors Association, 64

O

operating budget, 4, 13

operating costs, 9

operational problems, 55

operational records, 10

ordering (*see* purchasing)

organizational cost, 73

overtime, 169

P

par stock, 67, 68, 75–77, 92–93, 136

par stock method, 75

payroll cost, 153, 154–56, 158, 160, 163–65, 167, 170

daily fixed payroll cost, 156, 165

daily variable payroll cost, 156, 164, 165

estimated daily payroll cost percentage, 156

payroll dollars, 160–61, 163–64, 169

payroll software, 168

payroll tax, 155

perishable goods, 73–74, 103

person-hours, 175–76, 178

personal check, 140–41

bad checks, 140–41

check approval service, 140–41

pest control, 73, 91

plate presentation, 134

point-of-sale (POS) system, 10, 75–76, 136, 138–39, 140, 141, 144, 159

popularity, 50

portion, 118–120, 122

portion cost, 122

portion size, 29, 54, 77, 122, 131–134

standard portion cost, 30, 33, 35, 37, 44, 46, 50

portion control, 80, 131–36

preportioned item, 132, 134

portion control devices, 132–34

ladle, 133

portion scale, 134, 135

scoop, 132–33, 135

serving dish, 133

bowl, 133

cup, 133

individual casserole, 133

ramekin, 133

vegetable serving dish, 133

serving spoon, 133

price (*see* menu price, product cost)

price comparison, 69

price-value relationship, 48, 50, 54

"price wars," 47

pricing, 5, 23, 43, 47, 48, 50, 53, 54, 95, 97–100

competitive pricing, 47–48

prime cost, 9

product (*see also* menu item), 19, 29–37, 63–71, 73–80, 82–83, 89–94, 96, 100, 104, 105, 111–14, 116, 118–120

retail value, 80

product cost, 67–69, 71–73, 97, 99

product integrity, 89

product usage report, 136, 137

production, 9, 29–37, 112–16, 118–120, 122, 131–36

production quantity, 112–15

productivity, 170, 174–76, 178

profit, 3, 4, 10–12, 24, 36, 43, 44, 46, 68, 83, 89, 90, 105, 111, 116, 157–59, 166, 170

profit and loss report (*see* income statement)

profitability, 3, 10, 12, 157, 174

purchase factor, 77

purchase order, 64–66, 69, 82–83

purchasing, 62–84, 89, 90, 93

commissary, 69

competitive quotes, 67, 71

cost-plus, 68

frequency, 73

one-stop shop, 68

order quantities, 77–78

purchasing methods, 66–69, 71

sealed bids, 68–69, 71

standing order, 67–68, 74

purchasing agent (*see* buyer)

Q

quality, 12, 30, 48, 62–64, 67–68, 73, 74, 82–83, 89–92, 111–12, 136, 158, 166, 173, 174, 178

quote, 67, 71

R

receiver (*see* receiving clerk)